New Walks
in the
Yorkshire Dales

Jack Sharp was born in Wharfedale in 1932, and spent his early working life in the Bradford district in the dyeing industry, a subject on which he now lectures at Leicester Polytechnic. Like many Yorkshiremen who no longer live in the county, Jack Sharp likes to return to the Dales as often as he can. He has completed many of the most challenging walks in the district and has known the area all his life.

He lives in Leicester and is married with two daughters.

New Walks
in the
Yorkshire Dales

JACK SHARP

ROBERT HALE · LONDON

© Jack Sharp 1989
First published in Great Britain 1989

Robert Hale Limited
Clerkenwell House
Clerkenwell Green
London EC1R 0HT

British Library Cataloguing in Publication Data

Sharp, Jack
    New walks in the Yorkshire Dales.
    1. North Yorkshire Dales. Visitors' guides
    I. Title
    914.28′404858

    ISBN 0–7090–3816–X

Set in Times by
Derek Doyle & Associates, Mold, Clwyd.
Printed in Great Britain by
St Edmundsbury Press Ltd, Bury St Edmunds, Suffolk.
Bound by WBC Bookbinders Limited.

Contents

All maps were drawn by Ken Johnston

Foreword

The most popular walks in Yorkshire, the Three Peaks and the Lyke Wake Walk are suffering from erosion, due largely to overuse.

If the Dales are to cope with this large number of walkers it is essential that leisure seekers should spread themselves out a little more evenly. With this in mind I have compiled and completed walks in the Dales National Park and surrounding area. The total walking distance is over 500 miles. Each walk has a shorter alternative in the same area. Guides are provided for the walker to enable him to plan the intended route with the help of the appropriate Ordnance Survey map. No attempt has been made to produce a detailed guide which relies only on written instructions. How much more satisfaction can be gained on arrival at the intended destination after skilful use of map and compass.

Distances are approximate and recorded in miles and kilometres. Occasionally in the directions I have used metric units only. This is for convenience and refers to the grid lines on the map which are one kilometre apart. Heights climbed are recorded in feet and estimated from the O.S.map.

I hope that all readers get as much pleasure out of planning and walking these routes as I have had in devising them.

Preface: Safety

It is 3.30 p.m. on a bright sunny day in February. The lone walker has had a tiring but very satisfying day walking on the tops. He has finished his food and hot drinks. In an hour he will be back at the car in the valley bottom, and in two hours he will be lying in a hot bath reflecting on an exhilarating day's walk. He slips on an ice-covered rock and breaks his ankle. What can he do? No one to help him, no food, no hot drinks, no survival bag. In an hour's time there will be 6°F of frost. Will he survive the night?

A very dangerous situation. How could it have been avoided? By observing a few simple safety rules:

- In winter, never walk alone in the hills. A minimum number is four people. Then, if a member of the party has an accident, another walker can stay with him to keep him warm whilst the other two members go for help.

- Before starting a walk tell someone your route and expected time of completion. If you are long overdue a search party can be arranged.

- Never allow yourself to get over-tired when walking. Divide a long walk into short sections. Always be sure in your own mind that you can finish a section and be safely back in the valley and civilization without undue exertion.

- Think of possible escape routes from the tops before starting a walk.

- Aim to finish a walk with emergency rations and some drinks still available.

- Carry recommended equipment.

Accidents such as this can and do happen. If the walker disregards safety his chances of survival are slim. On the other hand, if he has taken all the necessary precautions, help will be immediately at hand from his companions and he will be kept warm and comfortable until a rescue party arrives.

Equipment to be carried when walking

    Ordnance Survey map of the area
    Compass
    Walking boots
    Sweater
    Suitable trousers (not jeans)
    Waterproof over-trousers
    Waterproof cagoule
    Woolly hat
    Gloves
    Survival bag
    Whistle
    Mug
    Emergency rations and Water
    Torch with spare batteries
    Small change for telephone calls

Weather

The weather can change very rapidly in mountainous regions, sometimes without warning. I remember an occasion in Wharfedale when at lunchtime it was too hot and sunny to sit outside the pub at Kettlewell, yet an hour-and-a-half later a thunderstorm was approaching over the top of Great Whernside. I had to abandon a walk on the tops to head for the comparative shelter of the valley. It would be foolish to carry on walking on the tops in a thunderstorm.

A figure, or group of figures, on an exposed landscape would form the ideal point source for a flash of lightning to run to earth.

Cold can be another killer in the mountains. Regrettably many people die in our mountain regions each year. Many of these deaths could be avoided by people taking advice not to walk and climb in the mountains in the worst of our winter weather.

The temperature drop is on average 0.6°C per 100 metres climb (i.e. about 3°F per 1,000 feet). This is compounded by the wind-chill factor, as the wind speed will be greater at higher altitude.

The effects of wind-chill cannot be over-emphasized. It is quite possible to be climbing in winter and to become very warm due to exertion, yet to be shivering one minute after stopping. This can be prevented by not stopping on the summit of the hill. Walk over the top and down to a more sheltered area before taking a rest.

Even in Summer, a rest on the exposed top of a hill might result in cramp.

Clothing
Correct clothing is very important. Windproofs are a necessity.
In Winter, thermal underwear is also necessary.
The woolly hat prevents heat loss through the head.
Put on extra clothing when stopping for a rest.

Food and drink
Do not run out of food or drink. Emergency rations should be carried in addition to normal food requirements.

Kendal mint cake is a favourite; alternatives are fudge, chocolate bars, fruit pastilles, etc.

In hot weather drinks are more important than food. Loss of liquids by sweating must be replaced. That is why I have included a pub at lunch-time wherever possible. It is advisable

to buy drinks where possible and to conserve your own supplies
for that emergency occasion.

Footwear

Guides recommend walking boots with a good ankle support.
These are essential for the novice.

Experienced walkers are now favouring trainers, but this
increases the risk of ankle injury.

Map and compass

The walker should be proficient in the use of map and compass.

Silva compasses are very popular. They range in price from
about £6 up to about £25.

When following a route by compass bearing, the map must first
be set so that it is aligned relative to the ground, i.e. so that the
grid lines on the map are running north to south and east to
west. Hold the compass horizontally. Rotate the compass
through a horizontal plane until north on the compass needle
points towards the arrow on the casing. Holding the compass in
this position turn the circumference of the needle housing until
north is aligned with both magnetic north and the arrow. Rotate
the map until the north-south grid lines – Eastings – are parallel
with the edge of the compass.

For rough use of the compass this might be accurate enough.
However, it does not take into consideration the deviation of
magnetic north from true north. At present, magnetic north is
about 6° 30′ west of grid north. This magnitude of error in
direction of travel will produce a deviation of one eighth of a
mile after one mile walking.

To compensate for magnetic variation remember the mnemo-
nics MUGS and GUMA. (i.e. Magnetic unto Grid – Subtract,
and Grid unto Magnetic – Add.)

SETTING THE COMPASS

Once the map is set:

1. Lay the compass on the map so that the long edge of the compass is aligned to join your present position with your destination.
2. Turn the outer ring of the compass so that north lines up with magnetic north on the compass.
3. Keeping north on the compass in line with magnetic north, walk in the direction of the arrow on the front of the compass.
4. Once the direction has been established by the above technique look for a feature in the landscape which is lying in the intended direction, (it might be a wood, an outcrop of rock or a building). Walk towards that feature and when you reach it pick out another feature lying in the same direction. Make regular checks with the compass to confirm you are still walking in the intended direction.

POINTS TO NOTE WHEN WALKING ON A COMPASS BEARING

1. There will be no footpaths. This inevitably means the ground will be uneven, cutting down walking speeds considerably. If your walking speed on a footpath is 3 miles per hour expect this to be reduced to 2 miles per hour when walking on a compass bearing.
2. Watch out for hazards ahead, e.g. boggy areas or mountain tarns. If such an obstacle lies in your line of walking, pick out a feature in your intended direction beyond the hazard. Walk round the hazard and get on course again after the obstacle.
3. Do not attempt to walk long distances on a compass bearing. Not only is progress very slow, due to the unevenness of the ground, but it is also very tiring. I use a compass bearing to walk from one path to another and I try to limit the distance across rough ground to a maximum of about 1½ to 2 miles.
4. An occasional back-bearing on your starting point is a good

way of confirming that you are still walking on course. This technique can also be used when the landscape ahead is featureless, making it difficult to head for a given target.

The reading for the back-bearing will be the intended direction in degrees plus 180°.

TO FIND YOUR EXACT POSITION ON THE MAP

Take two recognizable features on the ground that you can also find on the map. Take a compass bearing on each to give a back-bearing from each. Your position is where the two lines intersect.

If you know you are on a particular path, one back-bearing from a known object is all that is necessary. The position is where the back-bearing intersects the path.

I have used this technique to pin-point my position on the map. It is surprising what a boost of confidence you get when you can confirm your position.

Walking Strategy

As I will outline further on, footpaths in the Dales have many origins: they may have been Roman roads, pack-horse routes, corpse ways between village and cemetery or paths between lead-mine and smelt mill. When a path is no longer used regularly, for example after the closing of a lead-mine, or when after the introduction of the turnpike roads the packhorse routes were no longer used regularly, the path will have become less well defined. It is not surprising therefore that a path marked on the map may not be visible on the ground. For this reason it is a good practice when following a path over the top to take a compass bearing of the destination in the next valley before walking uphill.

One learns to be able to pick an easier route cross-country. A footpath can often be found running by the side of a boundary wall or fence, and it is unlikely that a wall will go through the middle of a bog. There will always be a path between shooting butts; however it may be on private land.

The vegetation and rock type give a clue to potential hazards. An area on the map called a moss is likely to be dominated by cotton grass moss and be very boggy. This will occur in areas where the underlying rock is millstone grit, particularly at high altitude where leaching has degenerated the soil type, and on relatively flat areas where the surface water cannot drain away. On the other hand, limestone is indicative of a shallow, well-drained soil often with a springy turf which is a delight to walk on. It is therefore possible when aiming for a particular destination across a valley to pick out the best route by first observing the vegetation and rock types.

Heather moss is usually well drained and so unikely to be boggy, but the heather may be quite deep and difficult to walk in. Peat hags may be several feet deep and boggy, and crossing them is very tiring due to the continual scrambling up and down. A very bright yellow-green moss is indicative of boggy ground and should be avoided.

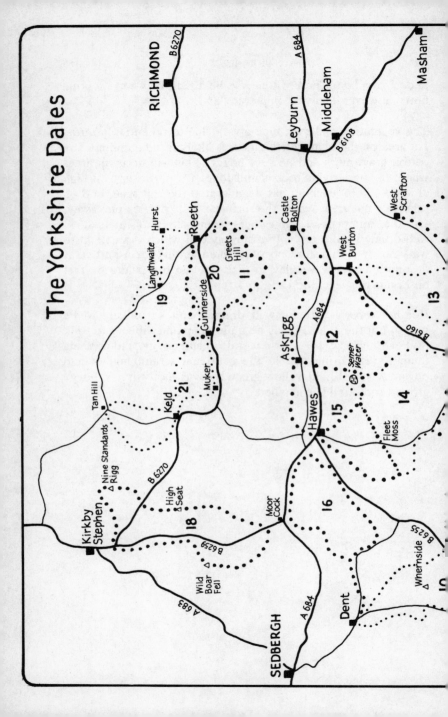

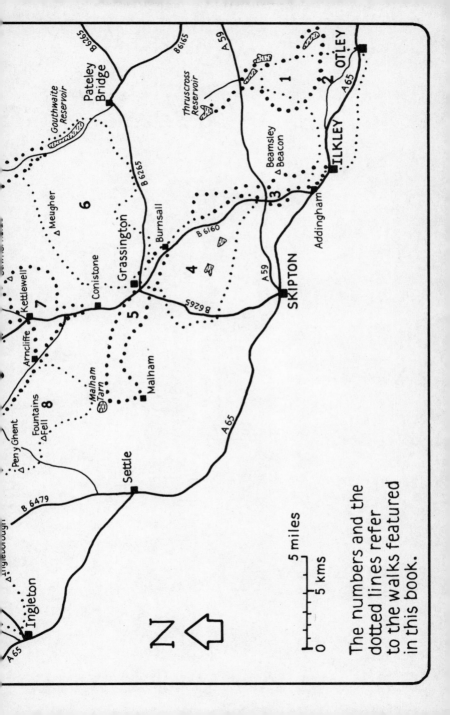

The numbers and the dotted lines refer to the walks featured in this book.

Introduction:

The Origins of Footpaths in the Dales

Prehistoric Routes

The existence of prehistoric paths in the Yorkshire Dales is purely conjectural: there is no documentary evidence to back them up. It is, however, likely that many tracks originated in prehistoric times, some probably dating back to the time when our ancestors were nomads.

The geological fault known as the Aire Gap, which divides the northern from the southern Pennines, has formed a natural route for trans-Pennine travel. It was used to transport tin, copper and gold in the Bronze Age from Ireland to Scandinavia. Seven centuries later it formed the natural route of the Vikings between their settlements in East Yorkshire and the Danish settlements in Ireland.

The stone circle at Yockenthwaite, dating from the middle Bronze Age (1600-1000BC), lies close to a footpath. Is it not possible that this path was on a trans-Pennine route 3,500 years ago?

The old road running due north from Kettlewell to Cam Head veers east as a track to join the new metalled road at grid ref. 990763, sheet 98. Before joining the road it passed through earthworks built by the Brigantes to defend the approaches to Coverdale from the Romans. This surely indicates that the track is pre-Roman.

Roman Roads

The reason that the Romans invaded Britain was to take advantage of its mineral wealth. After two brief visits to Britain

19

in 55 and 54BC, the Romans did not return again until AD43. They quickly established supremacy south of the Thames, but due to the difficulty of transport in hilly country, and the fierce opposition from the Brigantes, it was not until AD71 that the Romans were prepared to advance north from Chester and Lincoln to the hill country of the Pennines.

The intervening years were spent in consolidating their gains: building roads to transport men and equipment quickly to the scene of any insurrection, and putting down opposition in Wales and from the Iceni led by Boudicca in East Anglia.

Venutius, leader of the Brigantes, realized there would be a concerted attack by the Romans and chose to defend a site at Stanwick, 6 miles north of Richmond. This stood in the line of advance of the road north from York. The fort at Stanwick can still be seen today: it comprises an area of 850 acres enclosed by earth mounds, which in places are 20 feet high.

The Romans advanced on Stanwick before the defences had been finished and inflicted a crushing defeat on their enemy. This was to be the last resistance to the Romans. They were now able to extend their transport network. Both northbound roads were extended and they also built a road from Scotch Corner to Carlisle via Bowes and Brough.

The Dales area is contained within a rectangle of Roman roads bounded by Chester, Carlisle, Corbridge and York. Within this area a network of Roman roads is concentrated around Bainbridge in Wensleydale and Ilkley in Wharfedale. The Roman fort at Bainbridge dates from the end of the first century AD. Pottery recovered from the site suggests that it was occupied for the remainder of the Roman period.

There are two known Roman roads leading from Bainbridge, one heading south and the other south-west. The course of the road heading south can be traced for the first 8 miles until it enters Buckden in Wharfedale. Beyond this point it is lost, but it is thought to have continued to Ilkley. The Roman road heading south-west can be traced on the map. It eventually reached Ingleton. It is thought likely that there might have been a road heading east from Bainbridge to link up with the Roman road from York to the north. No such road has been found, but it is interesting to speculate as to the course of such a road.

The Roman Fort at Ilkley lay to the south of the river near the site of the church. Roman tombstones are on display in the manor house at the side of the church. Ilkley was probably chosen for the purpose of guarding the Aire Gap: indeed, it was very important strategically to the Romans. No less than five roads radiate from its centre. These roads headed north to Bainbridge, north-east to Aldborough, east to Tadcaster, south-west to Manchester, and north-west to Overburrow and on to Carlisle.

Mastiles Lane on Malham Moor which heads east from Malham Tarn to Kilnsey must be Roman. Evidence supporting this is the site of the Roman camp at grid ref. 915655 and Street Gate at grid ref. 906656 – Street being derived from the Latin word *Strata*.

Monastic Routes

Granges developed as a result of endowments of land to a monastery by local landlords, who admired the piety of the monks. In exchange, they expected to receive favours in the afterlife for their generosity. These granges were farms in outlying districts, often many miles away from the mother church. For instance, Furness Abbey in Cumbria had as many as eighteen granges.

The Cellarer supervised the running of the granges but the day-to-day management was in the hands of lay brethren. Land held by the grange was too large to be worked by the lay brethren, so it was let to local farmers who had to pay rent, in the form of tithes. Each farmer had to give one-tenth of his produce to the grange. The tithes were used to finance the running of the grange and the excess was taken back to the abbey. Thus there was a traffic of goods between grange and abbey, which produced well-defined tracks.

Both Bolton Priory and Fountains Abbey had a grange at Malham and monastic tracks between Malham and the two religious houses still exist. The tracks to Fountains Abbey head east towards Threshfield by two different routes through Bordley grid ref. 942648 and Lainger House grid ref. 951628.

Subordinate granges or lodges also developed, for instance, at Arncliffe and Darnbrook, and there is evidence of tracks between Malham and these two villages.

Kilnsey was the main centre for sheep-shearing (clipping) as can be seen from this account taken from Whitaker.

Edward Hodgson of Kilnesey husbandman in his 84th year, giving evidence in 1579 relating to the payment of tithes of wool, said

> That he knew the Abbaye of Fountance and ye abbots there of for thirty yeres space next before it was supressed; who occupied the groundes called Fountance Felles; and further saith that ev're yere for 30 yeres space next before the s'd abbey was supp'sed the flockes of shepe which depastured on Fountance Felles were brought from thence to Kilnesey, where they were yerely clipped, and the wool carryed away from thence in waynes to Fountance Abbay.

The sheep were driven from Fountains Fell to Kilnsey along Mastiles Lane before shearing.

A wain was a carriage drawn by oxen, thus indicating that the roads from Kilnsey were good enough for wheeled traffic.

Sheep were driven many miles between their summer and winter pastures. It was the practice to graze sheep on low-lying land in winter and to take them to the fells in the summer. The Craven uplands were used from Ellenmas (3 May) to Michaelmas (29 September). Both summer and winter keepers had to appear at the annual audit before Christmas. From the evidence contained in the Fountains Abbey stock book it is possible to deduce the movement of sheep between their summer and winter quarters. A wether flock (castrated rams) numbering about 300 were wintered at Bollershaw, now called

High and Low Bishopside, near Pateley Bridge. They were
taken in summer to Darnbrook. A possible route would be
Pateley Bridge-Greenhow-Hebden-Threshfield-Mastiles Lane-
Malham Tarn-Darnbrook, which is a distance of over 20 miles.
A wether flock wintered at Braisty Wood near Summerbridge
in Nidderdale (grid ref. 207636 sheet 99) was pastured in
summer on Malham Moor at Bordley Hall (grid ref. 942639), a
distance of 18 miles. Two remarkable journeys, both because of
the distances covered to take the sheep to their summer
pastures and, more particularly, because of the wildness of the
country through which they had to pass.

Sheep-rearing activities of the monks therefore contributed
to the development of footpaths in no small way.

Corpse Ways

Rural parishes in the Dales are very large, as a result of which
many people lived several miles away from the parish church.
This necessitated long journeys by the bearers taking their dead
for burial.

In Swalesdale the whole of the upper dale was served by the
parish church at Grinton. A death at Keld required a journey of
over 15 miles, taking two days. The corpse way from Keld
followed the road leading south out of the village. It then took
the present-day footpath over Kisdon to Muker and crossed the
Swale 1 kilometre north of the village. It then headed east,
passing through Dyke Heads, Gunnerside, Blades, Reeth and
Grinton.

In 1580 a new chapel and burial ground was consecrated at
Muker. Grinton continued to serve the dale up to Gunnerside,
but those who died above Gunnerside were buried at Muker. A
shorter corpse way connects Cotterdale with the church at
Lunds, which is situated near the source of the River Ure.

A hazardous journey for a funeral cortège was by the corpse
way connecting mid Wharfedale with Arncliffe in Littondale.
Before Hubberholme Church acquired its own burial ground,
bodies had to be transported from Buckden by the pack-horse
route – recognizable today by the hollow ways (paths worn into

a hollow by feet and hooves) – over Birks Fell, then carried up over 2,000 feet to cross Firth Fell and back down the steep descent of Ackerey Moor to Litton and then to Arncliffe. The bearers' task was to carry the corpse in a wicker basket, shoulder-high, up the steepest inclines and in all weathers, to its final resting place. To undertake such an arduous journey required a particular brand of strength and determination which we today find difficult to comprehend.

Pack-Horse Routes

Pack-horses were in use in the Bronze Age and probably date back to Neolithic times (before 2,000 BC). Their use developed in early monastic times and they served as the main means of transport for the next 600 years until the introduction of the turnpike roads in the eighteenth century. The two most popular breeds of pony used were the German Jaegar (hunter) and the Scottish Galloway.

Material carried by the horses was determined by local trade and included such varied items as lead, coal, corn, salt, wool and knitted stockings. A pony could carry about 100 kilograms (220 pounds) in a pair of panniers. The size of the load was relative to its density: lead, for example, was contained in small packs and wool in much larger ones. Ponies worked in teams of up to twenty or forty. The leading horse was decked in bells, both to keep the pack together and to warn other teams of their approach. The other ponies followed in single file, nose-to-tail. The sound of the bells must have been very familiar to the Dales people. Within living memory children in the Dales have played a game where they form a long crocodile lead by a child wearing a bell.

Each team of ponies was guided by one man, assisted by one or two boys. The guide was called a Jagger, after the German breed of horse. This name survives as a surname in the Bradford area. Alternative names for the leader were Brogger and Badger. A Brogger normally operated a pair of ponies collecting wool from farms for delivery to the clothiers in the West Riding. A Badger was a small trader who had a licence to carry corn between market and customer. This name survives in such placenames as Badger Way Stoop (grid ref. 065077, sheet 92) on Barringham Moor between Swaledale and Teesdale, and Badger Stone on Ilkley Moor (grid ref. 111461, sheet 104).

Pack-horse routes are common in the Lake District and the Yorkshire Dales. They are to be found in hilly country where passage by wheeled transport was impossible. Typically, a pack-horse route leaves a Dales village by climbing uphill and taking the shortest route. Often, on the steeper sections, the tracks will have been worn to a depth of 10-12 feet below the surrounding fields by the continual passage of feet and hoofs. These are the holloways or hollow ways. In extreme cases the pack-horses may have had to start a second track parallel to the first, and this has made a second hollow way.

The routes go over the tops from dale to dale. The route was simply a green track: it was not built, it just evolved due to the continual passage of foot and horse traffic. Stones were laid over the damp sections and the boggy areas were circumnavigated. In the valleys the larger rivers were crossed in shallow places by a ford and the tributary streams were often spanned by a pack-horse bridge. The Dales have many examples of pack-horse bridges. They were mostly built between 1650 and 1800. Multi-span bridges do exist, but the typical pack-horse bridge in the Dales is single-span and crosses a stream. It is very narrow and has a steep hump to keep it well above the level of the stream, even when in flood. Originally, the bridges had no parapets but these were added at a later date for safety.

Pack-horse routes connect village and market town or lead-mine to smelt mill: anywhere where large quantities of goods were carried between two centres. Arthur Rainstrick has estimated the volume of pack-horse traffic required for the operation of the lead-mines at Yarnbury above Grassington. By 1760 production of smelted lead had reached an annual figure of 600 tons, which meant that approximately 5,000 horse loads of lead had to be transported to market. In addition the dressed ore needed to be taken from the dressing floor to the smelt mill, which represented about 7,000 horse loads. Coal required for smelting the lead was calculated as 4,000 horse loads, and was transported from open-cast workings on the moors above Threshfield and Thorpe. This represented a total of 16,000 horse loads in a working year: that is, 50 loads for every day worked.

A similar problem occurred wherever lead was mined in large quantities: for example in the Swaledale-Arkengarthdale mining area. Transport became a big problem, and the only way to solve it was to make the roads fit to carry wheeled vehicles. The turnpike roads provided the answer.

I was walking along a footpath from Tan Hill to Raven Seat, when it occurred to me that this was an odd place to have such a path. Why was it there? After all, neither of these places are important. Later, I learnt that in the seventeenth century Lady Anne Clifford had a coal-mine at Tan Hill. She used the coal from Tan Hill for heating her castle at Pendragon, south of Kirkby Stephen. A close look at the map shows that this path heads in the direction of Pendragon Castle. The path was a pack-horse route. This can be confirmed by the pack-horse bridge at Raven Seat.

The diary of Lady Anne Clifford contains accounts of her expenditure whilst at Appleby Castle. In a seventeen-day period she paid for seven score and ten loads of coal: that is 150 loads in seventeen days, or nine pack-horse journeys a day in both directions.

If we can assume that Pendragon Castle required as much coal to heat it as Appleby, then this volume of horse-traffic between Pendragon and Tan Hill would soon make a well-defined track.

The Drove Roads

Drove roads were used to take animals to market on the hoof. Cattle, sheep, geese and horses were moved in this way.

It is likely that the movement of animals in herds goes back to prehistoric and Roman times. The practice was certainly used in monastic times. A letter surviving from 1359 grants two Scottish drovers safe conduct through England for themselves, their helpers and their horses, oxen and cows.

A drover might often have had over £1,000-worth of cattle on the move at one time. Carrying money in the form of cattle was much safer than carrying cash. The drover was quick to realize this, and acted as a messenger for cash. Any sum of money which he was asked to deliver was left at home and he raised the cash by the sale of his animals.

The large-scale movement of cattle from Scotland to England did not begin until after the Border wars. As English towns grew in size it became impossible to satisfy the market with local cattle so they had to be brought from further afield.

Thomas Hurtley, a Malham Schoolmaster writing in 1786, refers to Mr Birtwistle, a Craven grazier, and the first man to travel to the Hebrides and the Western Isles in order to bring cattle to the Dales. He started this trade in 1745, and had 10,000 head of cattle on the road at any one time. They were brought to Great Close, a field of 732 acres south-east of Malham Tarn. Here they were allowed to graze on the lush grassland. When they had fattened a sale was arranged. The field frequently held 5,000 head of Scottish cattle at any one time, and as many as 20,000 head in one summer:

> Every herd enticed from their native soil and ushered into the fragrant pasture by the pipe of a Highland Orpheus.

Several other graziers brought cattle from northern Scotland to Lancashire and Yorkshire. It has been estimated that at the peak of the trade in about 1800, some 100,000 cattle were annually driven from Scotland to England. The cattle which were brought to Malham, and other centres in the Pennines, were purchased and fattened by English dealers to be resold in the Dales towns of Ripon, Masham and Skipton.

It is possible that a cow born on a Scottish island, started its long journey south by swimming the short distance across the sea to the mainland. It then followed drove roads to Carlisle, Malham, the Midlands and the South of England.

Thomas Hurtley suggests that the trade in Scottish cattle was partly responsible for the demise of the local long-horned Craven cattle.

Cattle had to be shod, which required a total of eight shoes per animal. Sheep walked unshod but geese had their feet protected by walking them through a mixture of tar, sand and sawdust.

A herd consisted of about 200 cattle or a flock of 2,000 sheep. The latter was divided into four flocks, each controlled by a drover and his dogs. The animals would travel in a long column. Animals were taken on conventional roads, but in order to avoid payment of the toll on the turnpikes, and to protect cultivated land in the villages, an upland route was followed wherever possible. This ensured adequate grazing.

The drovers tended to follow similar paths, where they knew they could find an inn for the night. They covered about 12 miles a day. Drovers inns still survive in the Dales. Some are now farmhouses. Examples are at Gearstones near Ribblehead, and at High Dyke near Moorcock (grid ref. 803943, sheet 98).

The drove roads followed a south to south-east direction through the Dales area. Cattle coming from Scotland passed through Carlisle, after which one of many routes taken could have been via Appleby and Kirkby Stephen; then, following the west side of the River Eden, south to Wharton Hall and Lammerside Castle, probably crossing the Eden at Shoregill and following the route of Lady Anne Clifford to Hellgill (grid ref. 787967 sheet 98), High Dyke, (grid ref. 803943 sheet 98) south-east to Hawes then possibly Beckermonds, Halton Gill, Litton, Kilnsey and Skipton.

Droving has continued on a more localized basis within living memory. A local farmer recalls geese being taken on foot from Addingham to market at York, a distance of some 35 miles.

The advent of the railways and the turnpike roads heralded a new era of transport in the Dales. The old roads and tracks had outlived their purpose, but today they have once again come into their own. They are our legacy and remain simply for the pleasure of walking them.

The Walks

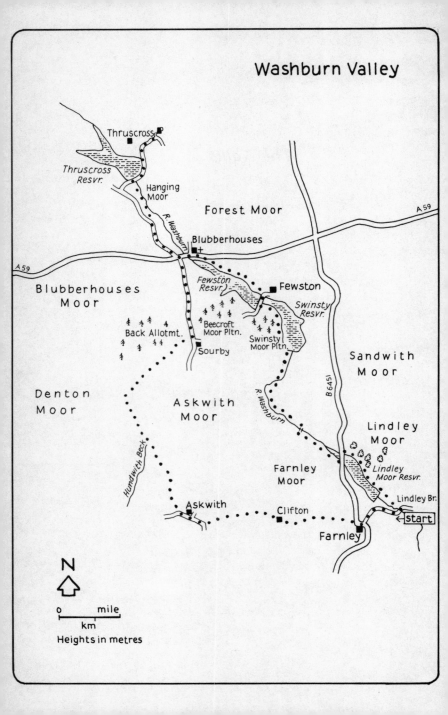

Walk 1: Washburn Valley

Lindley Bridge – Clifton – Askwith – Blubberhouses – Thruscross – Blubberhouses – Fewston – Swinsty – Lindley Bridge

36 km (22½ miles) / 1,300 ft climb

SHORTER ALTERNATIVE
22km (13¾ miles)

O.S. 1 in 50,000, sheet 104: Leeds, Bradford and Harrogate area

To drive to Lindley Bridge cross the bridge in Otley and take the first right turn following the B6451 round the back of Farnley Hall and turn left for Farnley. At the next left turn at grid ref. 216481 leave the B6451 to drive down to Lindley Bridge. Here there is sufficient space to park two or three cars off the road.

Having left the car, walk back up the road to the B6451, turn right (west) take the path at the side of the road to Farnley church for a quarter of a kilometre. Just above the church is a lane leading west to Haddockstones Farm. Follow this lane for three-quarters of a kilometre to where it takes a right-angle turn to the north, then leave the lane to continue walking west on the path that skirts the bottom of an L-shaped wood to join the Otley to Blubberhouses road at grid ref. 197484. Walk down the minor road to Clifton, take the path heading west past Covey Hall Farm and continue in a westerly direction to join a minor road at grid ref. 178482. Walk down this road and into Askwith; then, still continuing west, go past the turn-off to Blubberhouses and the Black Horse and at grid ref. 166484 take the minor road up to the right. Follow this metalled road – it eventually becomes a field path – to a farmhouse called Dunkirk at grid ref. 155509. Here, two paths diverge: one heads north-north-east, but this is difficult to find, so it is better to follow the path that heads just north of west to join a more defined path at grid ref. 150509. Turn right and follow this path first north, then north-east to intersect the Timble Ings to Timble road near Sourby. At the road junction (grid ref. 170531) turn left (north) and walk 2¼ kilometres down the road to its junction with the A59 in Blubberhouses.

Cross over the main road and follow the minor road opposite for about 2 kilometres to a point at the side of the road (grid ref. 157567) where a path follows the stream up to the dam of the Thruscross Reservoir. This path brings you up to the road, and through the car park, where the road can be followed for 2 kilometres, around the east side of the reservoir, up to the road junction (grid ref. 160587) and to the Stonehouse pub for lunch. I would not advise any attempt to walk round Thruscross Reservoir, even on the footpaths, because these are poorly defined and hard to find; as a result a long diversion by road is necessary.

Thruscross Reservoir was built in the late 1950s. While it was being built, part of the village of West End was submerged, including the pub and the cemetery. The bodies from the cemetery had to be exhumed and reburied in a place chosen by their relatives. A story circulating at the time claimed that the cemetery was surrounded by a temporary high fence and that work was only carried out after dark so as not to offend the residents. This macabre job was carried out by highly-paid volunteers.

After lunch it is necessary to retrace the route back to Blubberhouses; an alternative is to go straight down the more major road, but this is somewhat featureless and uninteresting.

The stretch of water below the dam is used for white-water canoeing with the co-operation of the local water authority controlling the outflow from the dam.

When you reach Blubberhouses walk east by the side of the

A59 for about half a kilometre to a lay-by at the right-hand side of the road. Here a footpath goes through the wood to the edge of Fewston Reservoir then leads on to a minor road at the edge of the wood. Follow this road, then take the road over the dam between Fewston and Swinsty Reservoirs. Immediately over the dam turn left to follow the path alongside the west bank of Swinsty Reservoir. This path follows the River Washburn downstream past a pack-horse bridge in Norwood Bottom.

This part of Washburn Valley was the scene of an action taken against witchcraft in the early part of the seventeenth century.[1] Edward Fairfax, a relative of Lord Fairfax, the general in the Civil War, lived at Newhall, the site of which is now under Swinsty Reservoir. He accused seven local women of bewitching his two daughters. They were tried at York Assizes but his charge was thrown out. Later the same year they were again charged and acquitted at the direction of the judge. It must have required great courage for the judge to rule against a man whose family connections gave him great influence in the country.

Keep following this footpath alongside the river Washburn until it reaches the B6451 road at the north end of Lindley Reservoir. Here turn left (north) and cross the bridge to follow the footpath on the east side of the reservoir back to Lindley Bridge.

Lindley Bridge to Stonehouse	20 km	12½ miles
Stonehouse to Lindley Bridge	16 km	10 miles
Total	36 km	22½ miles

Shorter Alternative
Follow the route above until you reach the crossroads near Sourby (grid ref. 170531). Walk east on the minor road for 1 kilometre to the Timble Inn. After lunch take the track to Nether Timble and again follow the River Washburn back to Lindley Bridge.

Lindley Bridge to Timble	14 km	8¾ miles
Timble to Lindley Bridge	8 km	5 miles
Total	22 km	13¾ miles

Reference
1. Guy Ragland Phillips, *Brigantia* (Routledge and Kegan Paul, 1976).

Walk 2: Wharfedale

**Burley – Chevin – Otley – Timble – Middleton –
Addingham – Ilkley – Burley**

41 km (25 miles) / 2,200 ft climb

SHORTER ALTERNATIVE
18½ km (11½ miles)

O.S. 1 in 50,000, sheet 104: Leeds Bradford and
Harrogate area.

This walk goes through the centre of both Otley and Ilkley, and
includes part of the Washburn Valley and Ilkley Moor.

A selection of places to park the car can be found on Ilkley
Moor, Burley Woodhead, Menston, etc. My choice was
Menston Old Lane in Burley (grid ref. 169452) at the crossroads
with Endor Crescent and Holme Grove.

Walk up Menston Old Lane to the point where the road
crosses the railway bridge, then after a quarter of a kilometre
take the path to the left off the road leading to Menston Village
railway station. Cross over the foot-bridge, then turn right to
join the A65 at the roundabout at the Fox and Hounds (grid ref.
177443). Walk down the road towards Otley for a quarter of a
kilometre. Just past a mill on the right (Murphy's) take the
footpath to the right through the fields, heading east to join the
minor road from Chevin End to Otley (grid ref. 190444). Turn
left and walk downhill on the road. Take the first road junction
on the right and walk along Bird Cage Walk for about half a
kilometre then turn left, cross the footbridge over the bypass
and walk into Otley. Cross the road at the traffic lights to reach
the river and follow the road heading north out of Otley. About

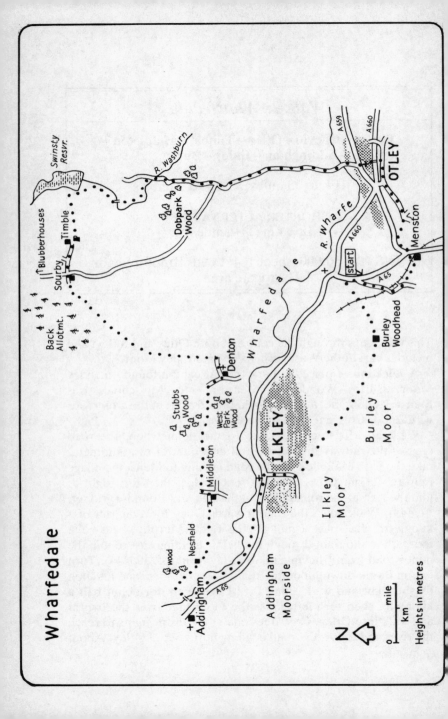

Wharfedale

Heights in metres

Swinsty Resvr.

R. Washburn

↑Blubberhouses

Timble

Sourby

Back Allotmt.

Dobpark Wood

OTLEY

A 659

A 660

Menston

A 660

R. Wharfe

start

A 65

Burley Woodhead

Wharfedale

Denton

Stubbs Wood

West Park Wood

Middleton

ILKLEY

Ilkley Moor

Burley Moor

Nesfield

wood

Addingham

A 65

Addingham Moorside

N

mile

km

0

3 kilometres from the town centre and still walking along the minor road, pass the turn-off to Clifton and the wireless masts, and at grid ref. 196487 leave the road to follow the footpath heading due north. This joins a minor road after 1 kilometre; follow this farm track north past Bride Cross House and Middle Farm, and down to the Pack-horse Bridge over the River Washburn (grid ref. 197509). Cross the bridge, turn left and follow the footpath which goes past the west side of Swinsty Reservoir. About half a kilometre beyond the dam wall, take the path on the left to Timble. The Timble Inn is a suitable stopping place for lunch.

From Timble walk west to cross the Otley to Blubberhouses Road, carry on past Sourby and, at the next junction of the path at grid ref. 164529, turn left at the signpost in the direction of Denton, Middleton and Ilkley. After about three-quarters of a kilometre, take the left-hand fork for Denton, as this path is more defined than the right-hand fork for Middleton. Walk the 4 kilometres over the moor to Denton. At the road junction in the village turn right and at grid ref. 141491 take the path to the left through the fields and Stubbs Wood to pass round the top side of Middleton Hospital. As you approach the hospital outbuildings take the right-hand fork in the path still following the footpath, to come out on the minor road at grid ref. 123494. Turn left and walk a quarter of a kilometre to the top of Curly Hill. Take the road heading west to High Austby (grid ref. 101494) where a path crosses the fields to Nesfield. Walk north-west on the road to a junction at grid ref. 085503. Turn left and walk past West Hall Farm and over the footbridge to the north end of Addingham. Turn left to follow the road towards Ilkley along Bark Lane. At the junction with the A65 (grid ref. 085495) follow the old road in a south-easterly direction. Just before this road rejoins the A65 turn left onto the path which follows the Dales Way back to Ilkley. Walk past the tennis courts in Ilkley and follow the path by the river to the Old Bridge, then the New Bridge at grid ref. 116480. Turn south and walk up Brook Street past the traffic lights towards White Wells, which is the white building on the moors

immediately ahead (grid ref. 118467). From here head
south-east passing on the low side of Ilkley Crags to follow the
footpath running parallel to, but above, the moor road from
Ilkley to Burley. This path leaves the moor at grid ref. 149446
where it joins a track leading down to the minor road at Burley
Woodhead (grid ref. 156444). Cross the road at this point to
follow the paths heading north-east, finally crossing the railway
line and returning to the starting point at the junction of
Menston Old Lane with Endor Crescent (grid ref. 169452).

Burley to Timble	14 km	8¾ miles
Timble to Addingham	14 km	8¾ miles
Addingham to Burley	13 km	8¼ miles
Total	41 km	25¾ miles

Shorter Alternative

Starting from Askwith follow the minor road towards Otley. At
the east end of the village (grid ref. 173481) take the track
leading off to the left, then the footpath to Clifton. Half a
kilometre beyond the village join the road from Otley, turn left
and follow the directions for the main walk through the
Washburn Valley to Timble.

From Timble, again follow the route as in the main walk but on
the path between Sourby and Denton turn left at grid ref.
150509 and walk half a kilometre east to a building called
Dunkirk. Here follow the path and minor farm road leading
south-east back to Askwith.

Askwith to Timble	10 km	6¼ miles
Timble to Askwith	8½ km	5¼ miles
Total	18½ km	11½ miles

Walk 3: Simon's Seat

Ilkley – Beamsley – Beamsley Beacon – Simon's Seat – Appletreewick – Barden – Bolton Abbey – Ilkley

40km (25 miles) / 2,260 ft climb

SHORTER ALTERNATIVES
1. 16½ km (10¼ miles)
2. 14½km (9 miles)

O.S. 1 in 50,000, sheet 104: Leeds, Bradford and Harrogate area. Appletreewick is not on sheet 104. It is just on sheet 98 but it is not necessary to carry the map for this very small section of the walk. This walk is not completely covered by the O.S. 1 in 25,000 Leisure Series.

When you reach Ilkley, walk down Brook Street to the church on the A65, then continue down the road to the New Bridge over the river Wharfe.

Immediately over the bridge turn left and follow the path along the riverside to the Old Bridge, then follow the road up to Middleton Lodge. At the road junction (grid ref. 112492) continue up the hill in a northerly direction to a bend in the road at grid ref. 113499. Here take the field path heading north-north-east for half a kilometre until you reach the open moor. Once on the moor, take the right-hand of the two paths that goes to Wards End (grid ref. 105517). Follow the path to the west until it joins the road again just south of Beacon Hill House, then follow the road north-west to the edge of the National Park boundary. From here a well-defined path leads to the Triangulation point (or trig point, the point of reference for

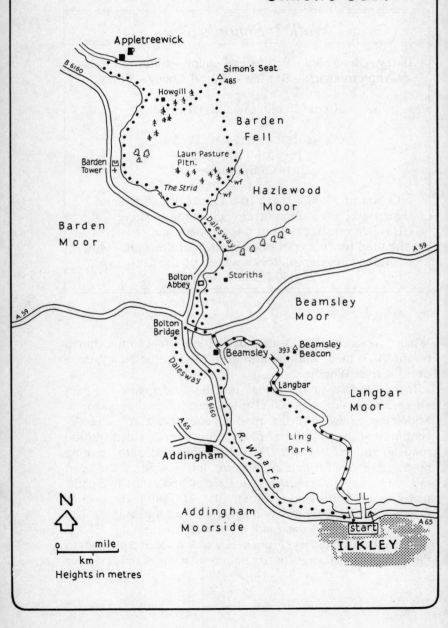

the height of the hill), on Beamsley Beacon. From here you can
see Chelker Reservoir on the Ilkley to Skipton road, the valley
of the Wharfe near Bolton Abbey, and Simon's Seat in the
distance towards the north-west.

The Bolton Abbey registers for 1803 states: 'Apprehensive of
a French Invasion, Beamsley Beacon was put in a state of repair
and four people appointed to watch it'.[1] Thus, in the event of
hostilities, the country could be alerted by a chain of beacons,
and the volunteers would be ready to fight off the invaders.

Retrace your route back to the road then follow the road to
Beamsley and join the A59 near Bolton Bridge (grid ref.
077528). Turn left and walk half a kilometre to Bolton Bridge.
Just before the bridge turn right through a cottage yard on a
path which follows the east bank of the Wharfe upstream to
Bolton Abbey and on to Cavendish cafe and the footbridge at
grid ref. 077553. Still keeping to the east bank of the river, walk
upstream from the bridge for about one-third of a kilometre to
the top of the little hill and follow the footpath across the fields
by the side of a house. The path leads north away from the
Wharfe through the Valley of Desolation, so named after a
storm in about 1830 which uprooted many trees. Today,
however, one of the features of the valley is the number of oak
trees still standing and the great number of young oak trees
which have recently been planted.

Cross the stream just below the bottom waterfall, then strike
up through the wood – Laund Pasture Plantation – to the open
moors. The track on the moors is well-defined and easy to
follow through the heather and bilberries to Simon's Seat. This
is a grouse moor and, although there is a public right-of-way,
the moors are private and therefore it is important to stay on
the paths. The moors may be closed to the public during the
grouse shooting season: this starts on the 'Glorious Twelfth', so
the second half of August in particular should be avoided for
walking on grouse moors.

Many distinguished visitors have been invited to shooting
parties organized by the Dukes of Devonshire on these moors.
Among the guests have been King George V (on fourteen

occasions) and Harold Macmillan during his term as Prime Minister.

Simon's Seat consists of a large outcrop of millstone grit. There is a good view of Upper Wharfedale from the summit. It is not necessary to retrace your steps as another footpath is signposted from Simon's Seat to Howgill. Follow this until you reach a cleft in the hill where Howgill runs down to the Wharfe. The path turns more steeply downhill and can be followed back to the river.

When you reach the bridge over Howgill (grid ref. 060593), take the path on the north side of this bridge back to the river Wharfe and follow the path upstream on the east side of the river to the path that crosses the fields to Appletreewick at grid ref. 052598. Appletreewick is just off the map (sheet 104). This path joins the road through Appletreewick opposite the New Inn, or if you want to try an alternative pub, the Craven Arms is 200-300 metres along the road to the left in the direction of Burnsall.

Appletreewick's claim to fame is that it was the birthplace of Sir William Craven. He is reputed to have entered London shoeless and penniless, yet he rose to become sheriff in 1600-1601. He built Burnsall Grammar School.

In 1300 Appletreewick was purchased by the monks of Bolton Priory and there is a sum in the priory accounts of £34.13s for expenses incurred by the prior for a journey to Rome in order to purchase a bull for the village. In 1900 Speight estimated this sum to be worth £500, so by today's values it must be worth several thousand pounds, which indicates the lavish spending of the priory.

From Appletreewick it is necessary to retrace the route back to the river Wharfe, then walk downstream to Ilkley. The footpath runs along the east bank of the river to Barden Bridge, where there is a path on both sides of the river to Bolton Bridge. From Bolton Bridge turn right on to the road and walk to the junction of the Harrogate to Skipton road with the road coming from Ilkley. Here, turn left towards Ilkley, then take the first turn on the right up a farm track and over the dismantled railway line to Hawpike farm at grid ref. 064526; then follow the track, turn left to Lobwood House (grid ref. 074517) and cross the B6160, following the Dales Way by the riverside, and join the road just before the church in Addingham (grid ref. 085497). Follow the minor road to its junction with the A65 Ilkley to Skipton road; then take the old road which runs parallel with the new one. Just before these two roads join again at grid ref. 093483 follow the path along the river bank which passes Ilkley Tennis Club and continue to the New Bridge in Ilkley.

Ilkley to Appletreewick	22 km	13¾ miles
Appletreewick to Ilkley	18 km	11¼ miles
Total	40 km	25 miles

Shorter Alternatives

1. Start and finish at Cavendish Cafe, Bolton Abbey, using the same route as in the above walk, i.e. Valley of Desolation, Simon's Seat, Howgill, Appletreewick, then downriver to Bolton Abbey.

Cavendish Cafe to Appletreewick	9 km	5½ miles
Appletreewick to Cavendish Cafe	7½ km	4¾ miles
Total	16½ km	10¼ miles

2. Service buses run from Ilkley to Grassington. Park the car at Bolton Abbey in time to catch the bus up to Grassington, then return on the footpaths by the side of the Wharfe to Bolton Abbey.

Grassington to Bolton Abbey	14½ km	9 miles

Reference
1. Harry Speight, *Upper Wharfedale* (Elliot and Stock, 1900)

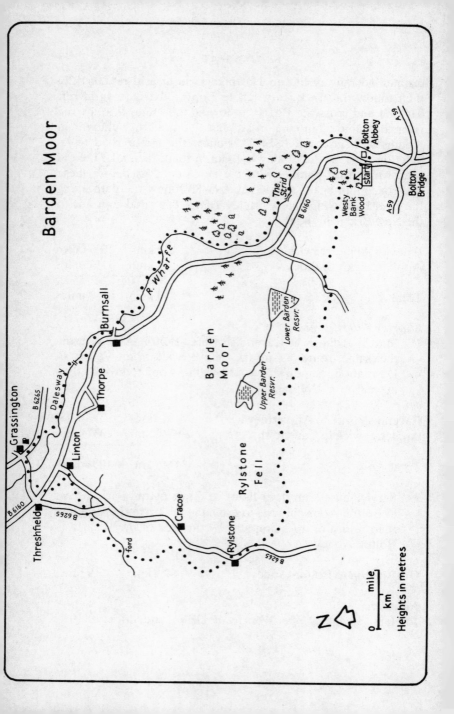

Walk 4: Barden Moor

**Bolton Abbey – Barden Moor – Rylstone – Linton –
Grassington – Bolton Abbey**

39 km (24½ miles) / 1,700 ft climb

SHORTER ALTERNATIVES
1. 33 km (20½ miles)
2. 13 km (8 miles)

This walk requires 3 sheets of the O.S. 1 in 50,000 to
cover it: sheets 98, 103 and 104, but the complete
walk is covered by O.S. 1 in 25,000, Outdoor Leisure
No. 10: Yorkshire Dales Southern area.

Park in the large car-park at Bolton Abbey. The first section of
the walk is a waymarked bridle-way which, in the main, is well
marked but inevitably the markers are missing in places. For
this reason it would be foolish to attempt this walk without
compass and map. It is interesting to speculate why this
well-defined track apparently heads nowhere of any importance. The clue must be its starting point, Bolton Abbey, as this
indicates that it is a monastic track. Bolton Abbey had a grange
at Malham and this could well have been a track used by the
canons and lay brothers when they travelled between the
priory and its grange. The track to Rylstone is in a direct line
with Malham, and at Rylstone there is a manor house which
could have been a halfway point for the canons on their
journey. Looking at the modern map a possible route from
Rylstone could have been via Hetton and Moor Lane to the
north end of the present Winterburn Reservoir and from here
to Hetton Common Head and Malham. It must be emphasized,
however, that this cannot be verified.

From the car-park take the road towards the Priory. Go through the Three Arches, the aqueduct which carried water to the priory. Immediately beyond the Arches follow the bridle-way which is signposted to the left heading up hill from the road.

On leaving the road one immediately gets a feeling of peace and tranquility away from the crowds. There is still a small pond by the path which must have been used for breeding fish during the heyday of the priory. After going through the wood the path emerges on to the open moors and affords magnificent views of Barden Tower and Wharfedale from an unusual angle. On reaching the minor road at grid ref. 037556 take the track heading west; join the bridle-way after half a kilometre, then follow the waymarked route towards Rylstone. I found it necessary to consult map and compass occasionally to check the correct path. Continue across the moor on the bridle-way until it joins another track near Bark Brow (grid ref. 973576). Here turn right (north) and follow this path for a quarter of a kilometre until it veers north-west; there take the path across the fields to come out in Rylstone near the church, turn left and walk past the manor house to the main road, the B6265. Take great care, as the lorries using this road to and from Swinden Limestone Quarry are prone to travel very fast.

Turn right and follow the road for 100 to 200 metres until the road bears right. In a lay-by on the left-hand side of the road; a sign-post points up Mucky Lane. Follow this track for 1 kilometre until it joins a minor road at grid ref. 966594. Turn right and follow this road to its junction with the B6265, then turn left and follow the track north-west along a walled lane and eventually up Swinden Lane. After a short distance the track crosses open fields and, as it is hard to follow, a compass bearing may be necessary. You are heading for the ford at grid ref. 973616. Just beyond the ford another path is intersected: turn right and follow this path in a north-easterly direction behind Swinden Quarry. (Surprisingly the activities of the quarry cannot be heard from here.) This path crosses open moorland, then continues down a walled lane to reach the

B6265 at grid ref. 985623. Here, cross the road once more and take the footpath immediately opposite, which leads into Linton. From Linton take the path over the fields towards Threshfield. This joins the Burnsall to Threshfield road at grid ref. 993635 where it is possible to take another path to join the B6265 and to make the final kilometre walk into Grassington.

After lunch, perhaps at The Devonshire, walk back to the B6265 and turn left towards Pately Bridge to enter the Yorkshire Dales car-park. At the bottom left-hand side of the car-park follow Sedber Lane to the River Wharfe, turn left and walk downstream on the Dales Way to Burnsall. Continue downstream to Barden where there is a choice of paths on either bank of the river back to Bolton Abbey.

Bolton Abbey via Barden Moor to Grassington	23 km	14½ miles
Grassington via river Wharfe to Bolton Abbey	16 km	10 miles
Total	39 km	24½ miles

Shorter Alternatives

1. Follow the route as above to Rylstone church, then walk round the right-hand side of the church up Chapel Lane to Cracoe. Here it is necessary to walk 1 kilometre north-east on the B6265 (take care) and at the point where the road turns north at grid ref. 983604, follow the minor road towards Thorpe, taking to the fields again at grid ref. 996612.

    This path is waymarked to Thorpe, then take the field path to Burnsall where it is again possible to follow the river downstream to Bolton Abbey.

Bolton Abbey to Burnsall	21 km	13 miles
Burnsall to Bolton Abbey	12 km	7½ miles
Total	33 km	20½ miles

2. From Bolton Abbey take the bridle-way to the cattle grid on the road at grid ref. 038556, turn right and walk 2½ kilometres on the road to Barden Bridge where paths on either side of the river go downstream to Bolton Abbey.

   Total   13 km   8 miles

Walk 5: Malham Tarn

Grassington – Burnsall – Thorpe – Linton – Bordley – Malham – Mastiles Lane – Threshfield – Grassington

40 km (25miles) / 1,500 ft climb

SHORTER ALTERNATIVES
1. 26 km (16¼ miles)
2. 10 km (6¼ miles)

O.S. 1 in 50,000, sheet 98: Wensleydale area, or
O.S. 1 in 25,000: Outdoor Leisure No.10: Yorkshire
Dales Southern area.

Park the car in the Yorkshire Dales car-park at Grassington. Take the footpath at the end of the car-park down to the river at the wear, turn left and follow the footpath down river passing the twelfth century Linton Church on the opposite bank, then a very pleasant walk down to the swing bridge close to Hebden. Here the footpath crosses the river and continues down to Burnsall along the other bank. The stone cliff at a bend in the river is called Loup Scar. This was the scene of a macabre incident in 1766.[1] The village blacksmith in Grassington was Tom Lee. He was a brawny man and a bully. Several robberies occurred in the neighbourhood and many people suspected Tom Lee as being the culprit but did not dare to name him. One day he lay in wait for the postman who travelled between Grassington and Greenhowe lead-mines. He attempted to rob the postman but got beaten up, and the postman escaped with the money. Lee went to Doctor Petty to have his wounds attended to. The Doctor suggested that Lee should mend his ways, and Lee, realizing that the Doctor now knew for certain

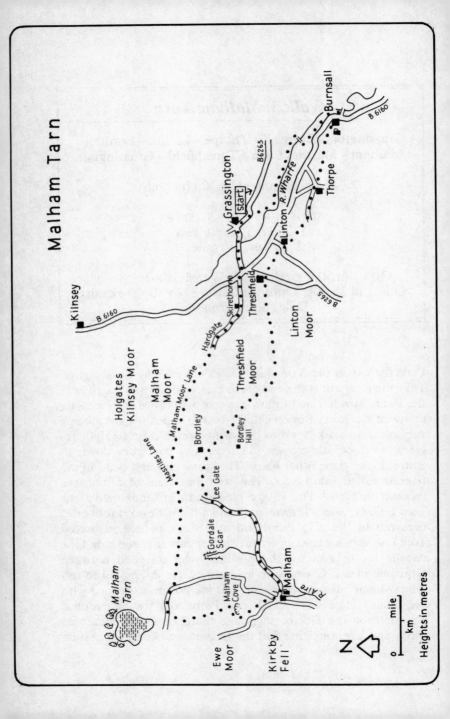

Malham Tarn

the identity of the local robber, vowed his revenge. The two later met in the Tennants Arms at Kilnsey. After the Doctor left the pub on horseback to attend to a patient at Conistone Tom Lee followed him and lay in wait for the Doctor in Grass Wood where he killed him. Lee hid the Doctor's body in some bracken, then later buried it on the moor, but when he discovered the preserving properties of peat, he returned a week later to retrieve the body and threw it over Loup Scar into the Wharfe, but he was seen by a courting couple, stood trial and was hanged for his crime.

From Loup Scar follow the river to Burnsall, turn right and walk past the Red Lion following the road up dale towards Grassington again. After the first bend in the road take the footpath over the fields to Thorpe. The route is well defined and easy to follow.

Thorpe lies in a hollow among the hills and cannot be seen from the Burnsall road. After the battle of Banockburn in 1314, when the Scots were raiding northern England and stealing cattle, they raided Bolton Abbey and Skipton. Thorpe was at the junction of these two routes. The local men hid their families and livestock in the village whilst they fought off the Scots, who never found the village.

In a nearby cave at Elbolton the skeletons of twelve human beings were discovered in the late nineteenth century. The skeletons are thought to be between two and three thousand years old.[2]

In Thorpe village take the left-hand fork in the road and at the southernmost point of the village turn right into Thorpe Lane leading in a south-west direction to join the minor road at Far Langerton (grid ref. 996612). Turn right and walk down the road for half a kilometre to the junction of a track at grid ref. 000617. Walk down this track to a barn, then turn right and follow the path over the fields to Linton. The large building on the left as you enter Linton is the 'hospital'.

Richard Fountaine, who lived in Linton travelled to London, where he made his fortune as a timber merchant and undertaker. When the plague came to London, Fountaine was taken ill but he miraculously recovered. This made him immune to the plague and the Government made him Undertaker-in-chief to the City. The poor were buried in pits and covered in quick-lime, but the wealthy were buried in private graves by the High Undertaker. Thus Richard Fountaine added to his fortune. He died in 1721 and the hospital was built out of a legacy left by him according to the terms of his will. The pub is also named after Richard Fountaine.[2]

Linton is one of the prettiest villages in the Yorkshire Dales with its three bridges straddling the beck: a footbridge, an old packhorse bridge, and the modern road bridge. No wonder the village was one of the early winners of the Yorkshire Dales best-kept village competition.

Walk down to the modern bridge and take the footpath by the side of the stream leading to Threshfield. Where the path divides take the left-hand fork over the old railway line to come out on the B6265 at grid ref. 988633. Go up the lane opposite which heads roughly west.

When you reach the open moor take the right-hand track for Bordley. This track is well defined and easy to follow. It eventually turns north as a green walled lane to the open moors, still heading north to Laithe at grid ref. 958646.

Here join the path heading west to Bordley, then after passing Bordley House Farm take the lane still heading west, eventually joining another lane at Lee Gate (grid ref. 926644). The metalled road can now be followed for about 4 kilometres to Malham.

According to Arthur Raistrick, the Malham – Gordale – Lee Gate – Bordley route was the main road going east connecting the Fountains Abbey properties. It continued to Skirethorns and Grassington.[3]

The Listers Arms in Malham was my lunchtime stopping place before setting off for the return journey back to Grassington. The problem is that all the routes up to Malham tarn are equally attractive and it is a case of which route to miss! After seeing Gordale Beck in flood I thought it would be foolish to attempt to scale Gordale Scar and I chose the route going up the west side of Malham Cove. This now has steps cut into the side of the cove to cut down the erosion.

The scenery in the Malham area is so dramatic that it is probably more attractive when it is raining than on a sunny day. After all, there is nothing more exhilarating than to see a mountain stream in flood, or to stand on top of the cove and catch an occasional glimpse of the valley below through a gap in the clouds.

The source of Malham Beck, which emerges from the base of the cove, was for many years a mystery. It was originally assumed to be from the Water Sinks just south of Malham Tarn, but it has been proved, however, by using tracer dyes, that the Beck's source is in fact the stream that drains into the ground at grid ref. 882659, and that the water sinks at the exit to the tarn (grid ref. 894654) and reappears at Aire Head (grid ref. 902622).[4]

From the top of the cove there are three footpaths going towards Malham Tarn. The Water Sinks are worth a visit and are particularly impressive in bad weather.

On reaching the road crossing the exit stream from Malham Tarn (Malham Water) turn east and walk for 1 kilometre until you reach a bend in the road where it turns south. Continue straight to Street Gate at grid ref. 905656: this is the start of Mastiles Lane. About one kilometre to the north of Street Gate is Great Close pasture, (732 acres) said to be one of the largest walled pastures in the north of England. In the mid-eighteenth century it was rented by a Skipton Grazier. Often there would be 5,000 head of Scottish cattle on this pasture at any one time. A fair would be held to sell the cattle, which would then be replaced by more cattle that would be grazed, fattened up and sold. Thus as many as 20,000 head of cattle may have changed hands in any one year on the pasture. The cattle came from as far afield as the West Highlands of Scotland and the Hebrides, being driven down the country on the drovers roads. The green roads that run roughly from north to south in the Dales are mainly drovers roads and those crossing the country are mainly roads between markets and were the pack horse routes. Up to

10,000 head of cattle would be on the move at any one time. It was this influx of large numbers of black cattle from Scotland that was probably responsible for the decline of the local long-horned craven cattle.

Sheep[3] and horses[5] were also grazed on Great Close pasture.

Mastiles Lane was built by the monks to take sheep to the annual sheep sales at Malham: the monks of Fountains Abbey were noted for their wool growing. A witness in a dispute in 1579 stated that he knew the abbots of Fountains for full thirty years before the dissolution. Every year the flocks of sheep were depastured on Fountains Fell and brought to Kilnsey where they were clipped and the wool was then carried away in wains to Fountains Abbey.[2]

Mastiles Lane starts as a grassy track with a wall on one side, then for about 1½ kilometres it runs between two walls before splitting into two tracks, one going to Kilnsey and the other heading south-east for Threshfield and Grassington. Follow the Grassington branch. The final 5 or 6 kilometres are on metalled road.

Grassington to Malham	24 km	15 miles
Malham to Grassington	16 km	10 miles
Total	40 km	25 miles

Shorter Alternatives

1. Park in Threshfield. Take the same route as above but missing out Grassington, Burnsall, Thorpe and Linton. The route is therefore Threshfield Lane Head, Laithe, Bordley, Malham and return via Malham Cove, Water Sinks, Street Gate, Mastiles Lane and back to Threshfield.

Threshfield to Malham	12 km	7½ miles
Malham to Threshfield	14 km	8¾ miles
Total	26 km	16¼ miles

2. A shorter walk which starts and finishes in Malham allows
    more leisured exploration of the local scenery. It is possible
    that the map of Malham and Malham Tarn area can be
    obtained cheaply in the Yorkshire Dales centre which is
    situated in the large car-park near Malham.

Leave Malham and head south-easterly along the footpath
which goes to Gordale Beck. On reaching the beck turn left
and follow the path to Janet's Foss, the waterfall below
Gordale Bridge, then follow the paths alongside Gordale
Beck up Gordale Scar. The climb up the waterfall is not too
difficult. Then head north-west on the path to Street Gate,
walk for 1 kilometre west on the road, then turn south on to
a footpath to pass the Water Sinks and return to Malham
Cove where there is a choice of paths back to Malham.

Total   10 km   6¼ miles

References

1. Halliwell Sutcliffe, *The Striding Dales* popular ed. (Warne, 1939).
2. Harry Speight, *Upper Wharfedale* (Elliot Stock, 1900).
3. Arthur Raistrick, *Malham and Malham Moor* (Dalesman, 1947).
4. Arthur Gemmell, *Malhamdale Footpath Map* (Yorkshire Dales National Park).
5. Arthur Raistrick, *Old Yorkshire Dales* (David & Charles, 1967).

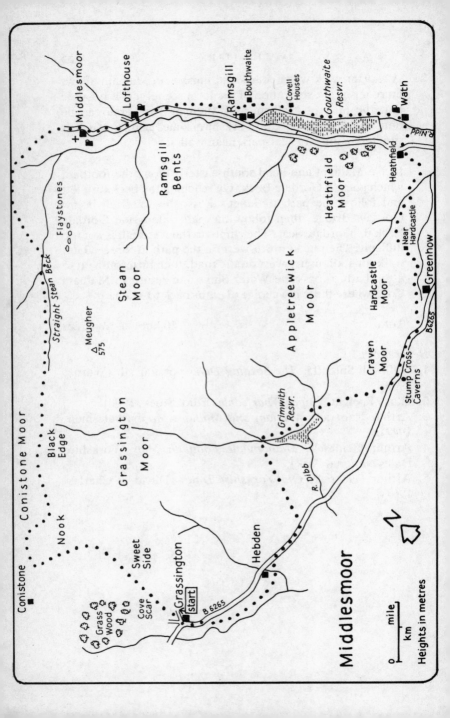

Middlesmoor

Walk 6: Middlesmoor

Grassington – Near Conistone – Watershed – Middlesmoor – Wath – Greenhow – Grimwith Reservoir – Grassington

49 km (30¾ miles) / 2,850 ft climb

SHORTER ALTERNATIVES
1. 17 km (10½ miles)
2. 7½ km (4½ miles)

The whole of this walk is covered by O.S. 1 in 50,000, sheet 98: Wensleydale and Wharfedale area, and O.S. 1 in 50,000, sheet 99: Northallerton and Ripon area.
Part of the walk is covered by O.S. 1 in 25,000 Outdoor Leisure No. 10: Yorkshire Dales Southern area.

This is a long walk, but a circuit from Grassington including upper Nidderdale and Gouthwaite Reservoir was difficult to plan to a shorter mileage. The route from Greenhow Village via Grimwith Reservoir and the river Wharfe is a circuitous route, but it avoids a long walk back to Grassington on the main road.

In Grassington a suitable place to park is the 'pay and display' car-park of the Yorkshire Dales National Park.

Walk to the village square in Grassington. Pass the Devonshire pub at the top left-hand side of the square then take the left of the two roads leading to the moors. Take the first road on the left, then look out for a signpost marked Conistone on the right, pointing through a farmyard, which is part of the Dales Way. This early part of the walk is on soft, well-drained, springy turf which is often found on limestone and is a delight to walk on.

Continue along the Dales Way to the junction of the track with Scot Gate Lane near Conistone at grid ref. 993683; then turn right up Bycliffe Road where it is signposted to Middlesmoor. This track roughly follows a north-easterly direction to the watershed.

At Mossdale Scar (grid ref. 017698) the path is poorly defined. (I missed the track and followed the line of grouse butts up from Mossdale Beck at grid ref. 022707, finally reaching the boundary fence at roughly the intended position. A compass reading on the only outstanding feature in sight, the peak of Meugher hill, confirmed my position.) From the boundary fence head north-east down Straight Stean Beck where the path is poorly defined. One can either follow Straight Stean Beck or take a slightly more northerly route which joins a minor road at Aygill Beck (sheet 99, grid ref. 060738) then follow this track, first north-east to Armathwaite Gill, then east and south-east to Middlesmoor.

As there is a pub in the village, it is a good place for the first stop. Alternatively, there is a pub at Lofthouse.

From Middlesmoor, a footpath leads directly to Lofthouse 1 kilometre over the fields. Follow the road down-dale out of Lofthouse for half a kilometre until it crosses Backstone Gill[1], then take the footpath to the right over the fields leading to Low Sikes. At this point the footpath is following the route of the dismantled railway. Do not attempt to follow the line from Lofthouse because the bridge across Backstone Gill has been removed!

From Low Sikes follow the waymarks of the Nidderdale Way. The path climbs up to the wood, follows its bottom edge to Bouthwaite then follows the waymarked path along the east side of Gouthwaite Reservoir. Notices request the walker to stick to the path and not approach the water because this is a bird reserve – nearly two hundred varieties of bird have been observed here.[1]

Gouthwaite reservoir which was completed in 1901, supplies water to Bradford. It is approximately 2 miles long and has a capacity of 1,565 million gallons. The old railway was built by Bradford Corporation after the completion of Gouthwaite Reservoir for the purpose of assisting construction of the other two reservoirs further up the dale. Angram was completed in 1919 and Scar House in 1936.[2] The Nidd Valley Light Railway ran from Pateley Bridge to Lofthouse as a daily service for members of the public as well as for the purpose of transporting both the workforce and materials to and from the reservoirs.

In monastic times Fountains Abbey and Byland Abbey owned land in the upper dale.[3] In the area bounded by the watershed to the west and north of the upper dale and on the south side by Stean Beck and by Backstone Gill to the east, Byland Abbey held the pasture rights and the monks were allowed to take wood from Backstone Beck wood for building their lodges and cattle folds.

The area to the west of the Nidd between Middlesmoor and the present position of Pateley Bridge was known as Stonebeck Down. It contained many granges of Byland Abbey including the following: Stean, Moor House, Blayshaw, Raygill House, Ramsgill, Colt House, Gouthwaite, Ashfold and Heathfield. To the east of the river the area was known as Fountains Earth and Fountains Abbey had granges at Thwaite, Thrope, Lofthouse, Sykes, Bouthwaite, Covell House, Holmehouse and Sigsworth. All of these placenames are on the present series of the O.S.1 in 50,000 map sheet 99, and the present walk passes through many of them.

At the south end of Gouthwaite Reservoir take the path down to the road across the dam but follow the path on the east side of the river down to Wath. Turn right on the road to join the main road up the dale at grid ref. 144677. Cross the road to take the path over the fields and uphill to Heathfield, then south-west to Westfield House and Ashfold Side Beck, joining the minor road at grid ref. 133665. Turn right (west) to follow the beck upstream. After crossing Rowantree Gill look out for a path down to the lead-mine ruins at grid ref. 119661. The path can now be followed up to Near Hardcastle, Brandstone Beck and then to Greenhow village on the B6265. Alternatively, from Brandstone Beck take the path heading south-west to join the main road about 1 kilometre west of Greenhow village. This will take you past the Sam Panty Oon Stone, an ancient grinding mill, and the Jackass Level at grid ref. 110646. Arthur Raistrick dates this level as being seventeenth century,[4] but it has been suggested that it might in fact be Roman.

In Greenhow Village follow the main road west towards Grassington, taking great care. After 2 kilometres you reach Stump Cross Caverns. Nearby Mungo Gill at grid ref. 091634 was the subject of a dispute between Fountains Abbey, Bolton Abbey and the stewards of the Forest of Knaresborough about 1480. This related to the ownership of the land and the mineral rights. The dispute was to continue intermittently for the next eighty years.

Beyond Stump Cross Caverns and after about a quarter of a kilometre, at a left-hand bend in the road take the signposted path to the right heading north-west to join the track going round the north side of Grimwith Reservoir. From the north-west corner of the reservoir walk south on the track (Hartington Moor Lane) to join the Pateley Bridge to Grassington Road at grid ref. 043631. Turn right and follow the road west for 1 kilometre to Bank Top, (grid ref. 033631); then take the footpath heading south-west to the suspension bridge over the Wharfe. Finally, follow the footpath west, on the north side of the river, back to Grassington.

Grassington to Middlesmoor	19 km	12 miles
Middlesmoor to Grassington	30 km	18¾ miles
Total	49 km	30¾ miles

Shorter Alternatives

1. From Appletreewick take the left-hand fork to Skyreholme. Beyond Skyreholme take the left fork to Parceval Hall. Just before entering the grounds of the Hall leave the metalled road to cross the fields to the left and walk through Trollers Gill. Note that it is possible to walk up the gill if

there is not too much water coming down. If the gill is in flood take the path to the left before you reach it. The gill is very pretty and worth the diversion. Whichever route is taken head for the road junction at grid ref. 060630, sheet 99. Here take the minor road north to go round Grimwith Reservoir anti-clockwise. From the north-west corner of the reservoir walk down the track leading south-west to the Grassington to Pateley Bridge Road, turn left and walk 1 kilometre to Dibble's Bridge. Cross the bridge and leave the road by a footpath on the right leading south over the fields to Appletreewick.

Total   17 km   10½ miles

2.   From Grassington park in the Dales car-park. Walk in to Grassington. From the square walk up the left-hand road beyond the Devonshire Hotel. Take the first road to the left, then follow the Dales Way through a farmyard on the right. After a short distance take a left fork in the path to go through Bastow Wood and Grass Wood, following the path going north-west, then west to join the Grassington to Conistone Road. Turn left and follow the road for half a kilometre towards Grassington, then take the path by the river and back to Grassington.

The best time to do this walk is in late spring or early summer when the great variety of flowers are at their best.

Total   7½ km   4½ miles

References

1. Maurice Colbeck, *Yorkshire, The Dales* (Batsford, 1979).
2. D.J. Croft, *The Nidd Valley Light Railway* (The Oakwood Press, 1987).
3. R. Fieldhouse and B. Jennings, *A History of Richmond and Swaledale* (Phillimore, 1978).
4. Arthur Raistrick, *Lead Mining in the Mid-Pennines* (D. Bradford Barton, 1973).

Great Whernside

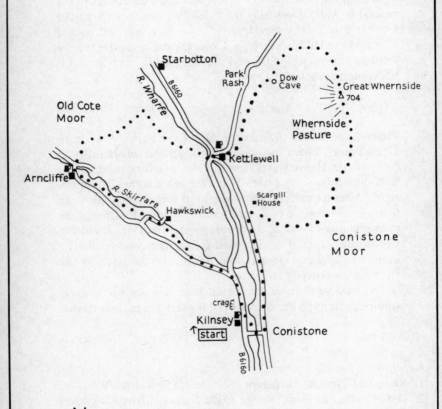

N

0 ___ mile

km

Heights in metres

Walk 7: Great Whernside

**Kilnsey – Arncliffe – Near Starbotton – Kettlewell –
Great Whernside – Conistone – Kilsney**

31½ km (19 miles) / 2,600 ft climb

SHORTER ALTERNATIVES
1. 16 km (10 miles)
2. 12½ km (8 miles)

O.S. 1 in 50,000, sheet 98: Wensleydale and
Wharfedale area

A convenient place to park the car can be found at the back of Kilnsey village approaching Mastiles Lane.

The most prominent feature in Kilnsey is the crag. It is 165 feet high and the overhang at the front is 40 feet. Because of it size and the overhang, the crag appears to be closer to the road than it really is. It is recognized as being quite an achievement to be able to throw a stone from the road to hit the crag. It is not impossible to do, but finding a stone of a suitable size in the vicinity is an achievement in itself! It is not surprising that such a dominant feature as Kilnsey crag should be used for a fell race in the annual show.

A more recent feature of Kilnsey, the trout farm, is man-made, but it blends in with the landscape very nicely. I am sure that the majority of visitors to the Dales, when they taste the local haute cuisine, will not realize that 'trout from Wharfedale' comes from the trout farm at Kilnsey.

A caravan once stood in a field near the site of the present trout farm until 1939. It had a German machine gun on its roof, a relic of the First World War, and had been exposed to the elements for many years. At the start of the Second World War this trophy was confiscated 'because it might be useful to an enemy'! – a likely story, since it must have been dropping to bits with corrosion.

The Old Hall or Manor House at Kilnsey is still in existence. One approaches it by taking the minor road from the side of the Tennants Arms towards Mastiles Lane. For many years it has been used as a farm building, but over one entrance are the initials CW and the date 1648. This was Christopher Wade. His son, Cuthbert, was a captain in the Royalist forces during the Civil War, but the most interesting point is the connection of this building with Lady Anne Clifford, who at the age of seventy-four stayed here as a guest of Cuthbert Wade in 1663, on one of her journeys north to Westmorland to visit her estates.[1]

On the moors behind Kilnsey is Douky Bottom Cave, where the remains of a Celtic infant were found. It was so small that the grave was no more than twelve inches long. Bone and bronze brooches have also been found, as well as flint implements and spindle whorls.

From the Tennants Arms at Kilnsey walk north up the road for 1 kilometre then take the left-hand fork going up Littondale for about one kilometre and branch right on to the path through the fields going towards Hawkswick. On reaching the metalled road, do not turn right into Hawkswick but stay on the same side of the river Skirfare following the road to the north west. After half a kilometre and before the road turns a right angle to the left, take the footpath which follows upstream to Arncliffe.

Here, you are surrounded by reminders of the history of the area. The river Skirfare gets its name from the Scandinavian Skirr, bright, clear, and Farr, meaning 'bright stream'. The contours in the fields supply a clue to their history: at Hawkswick the terraces sloping down to the village are Saxon cultivation ridges and the square lynchets above them are of celtic origin.[2] The height of the lynchets is in itself a clue to their great antiquity, because they were originally situated on the hillside; but when the lower slopes were cultivated the lynchets were abandoned for the richer soils of the valley bottoms.

Hawkswick was mentioned in Domesday. The names Hawkswick and Arncliffe both refer to birds of prey, Hawkswick being 'the village of the hawk' and Arncliffe deriving its name from the Anglo Saxon *earn* meaning eagle and *clyf* (a cliff). In 1294 the Abbot of Fountains Abbey gave Henry de Percy and his heirs the right to hunt wild beasts and birds of prey in Littondale.[1] This indicates that such animals lived in these parts at that time.

To the south-west of Arncliffe and at the side of Cowside Beck is Yew Cogar Scar, where yew trees grow between the limestone. There is a local tradition that the dalesmen cut the bows they used at Flodden in 1513 from these yews.[2] Maurice Colbeck states that Arncliffe provided five bowmen and three warriors equipped with 'billes' and that in all twenty-two men from Littondale went to the battle of Flodden.[3]

Arncliffe church must surely be in one of the most attractive settings of any church in the country in its position right on the banks of the River Skirfare. The best time of year to see the village is in early spring when the snowdrops and winter aconites are in flower.

At the west end of Arncliffe on Cowside Beck there was a corn mill in the fourteenth century owned by the canons of Bolton.[2] This property was mentioned in official documents at the time of Queen Elizabeth I and again in 1770. It was rebuilt in about 1790 as a cotton mill and finally closed in 1875. It has since been altered and is now a private house. Men from Kettlewell were employed in the mill and walked daily over Old Cote Moor to Arncliffe. I have often wondered about the origins of the paths over the hills in the Dales: here is one possible explanation of the path from Arncliffe to Kettlewell, or has it a much more ancient origin?

Charles Kingsley visited Arncliffe and it is thought that he started writing *The Water Babies* here.

Leave Arncliffe by the road towards Litton. After about a quarter of a kilometre one comes to a beautiful stone-built sixteenth-century farmhouse called Owlcotes. It is known to be sixteenth-century because it was one of the granges of

Fountains Abbey. In the twelfth and thirteenth centuries much of Craven passed into the possession of the monasteries, and Littondale was granted to Fountains and Salley. Other granges in Littondale were at Hawkswick, Hesleden and Cosh at the remote northern end of the dale.[4] Tradition says that the monks slept in an upper room above the porch at Owlcotes.[2] This house must therefore have been in existence before the dissolution of the monasteries in 1536.

The track from Owlcotes is followed over Old Cote Moor to Starbotton. Again, the well-defined track indicates much greater use in former times. This in fact was part of the vast network of green tracks in the uplands used as market routes by the pack-horsemen.

As mentioned earlier, pack-horses were the main means of transport for about five centuries. They had their origins at the time of the monasteries and only ceased to be the main means of transport when the present road system was built in the early nineteenth century. This particular section of track was part of the route from Settle in Ribblesdale to Nidderdale.

A careful look at the map shows this track partly following the course of modern roads and present-day footpaths from Settle to Langcliffe over Malham Moor along Cowside Beck to Arncliffe, across Old Cotes Moor to Starbotton and Cam Head, past the earthworks near Park Rash at Tor Dyke and crossing over to Nidderdale between Great and Little Whernside. So in fact what today is a little-used track frequented only by walkers was formerly a busy highway with teams of pack-horses traversing it. One of the features of the pack-horse routes that makes them easy to identify is the fact that the gradient of a hill was no problem to the ponies, and often these routes go straight up a hill where wheeled transport could not cope: the track from Arncliffe up to Old Cotes Moor is one such example.

Follow the track almost to Starbotton but before the final descent into the valley, above the tree line pick up a path going south-east to Kettlewell. Join the B6160 road near the new bridge over the Wharfe and walk into Kettlewell, where there is a choice of over three pubs for lunch: the Racehorses, the Blue

Bell, and the King's Head.

Leave the village on the track running north-north-east to Hay Tongue, or alternatively take the path towards Park Rash and follow Park Gill Beck to the earthworks marked on the O.S. map. This is Tor Dyke, a deep ditch excavated by the Brigantes, the indigenous population, as a second line of defence against the Romans in the event of an attack on their fortress at Stanwick.[6]

The road from Kettlewell to Wensleydale via Coverdale is a minor road today but it was a main highway in its day. It was on the Roman road from Bainbridge to Ilkley, and on the monastic way from Coverham Abbey, because Coverham, together with Bolton and Fountains Abbey, held land here.[4] Richard Neville, Earl of Warwick (Warwick the Kingmaker) held Middleham Castle as his favourite retreat and Richard III spent much of his early life at Middleham so one can imagine the Royal processions using this route through Coverdale to the north.

In monastic times the road took a slightly different route to its present one up Park Rash. It followed the walled track going due north from Kettlewell to Cam Head, then curled round to the east, joining the route of the present road to the north of Tor Dyke. Hunters stone, which lies slightly further north was a monastic cross built to guide the monks on their route from Kettlewell to Coverham.[2] The former route of the road from Kettlewell explains the reason for the position of the Brigantian earthworks.

In more recent times the road up Park Rash was on the route from Skipton to Richmond in the coaching days, but it was soon abandoned because of the difficulty of negotiating Park Rash with its gradient of 1 in 4 and acute bends. Even today, one requires a strong nerve when driving down the hill by modern car.

Dow cave, on a feeder stream to Park Gill Beck, is worth a small diversion. It is very popular with potholers and, unlike most potholes, the entrance is a gentle slope. It looks very inviting, but should only be entered by experts with the proper equipment.

From the earthworks a path can be followed to the east to the summit of Great Whernside.

In the thirteenth century the name Whernside was Qwernsyd and was derived from Cweorn (Old English) and Kvern (Scandinavian), meaning 'the hillside from which mill stones are derived'.[7] The millstone grit on the summit of the hill is the stone in question.

Follow the boundary to the south to grid ref. 030712 and join the path from the tops bearing south-west and following Mossdale Beck; then follow the track down to Conistone, cross the bridge over the Wharfe and take the path through the fields to Kilnsey.

Kilnsey to Kettlewell	12½ km	7 miles
Kettlewell to Kilnsey	19 km	12 miles
Total	31½ km	19 miles

Shorter Alternatives

1. Starting in Kettlewell take the old track leading due north out of the village to Cam Head. Take the track going north-east then east skirting the earthworks, and follow the district boundary to the summit of Great Whernside and the boundary south to grid ref. 006733. Leave the boundary and take the path from the summit back down to the minor road from Conistone to Kettlewell at grid ref. 976708, near Scargill House. Walk the final 2 kilometres back to Kettlewell on the road.

   The area around Park Rash is called Scale Park. In 1410 Henry IV granted a licence to Ralph, Earl of Westmorland to enclose 300 acres of land for a deer hunting park.[2]

Total	16 km	10 miles

2. From Kettlewell cross the river Wharfe by the road bridge, then follow the path on the west side of the Wharfe going north to Starbotton. Cross the river by the bridge and take

the old pack-horse track up to Cam Head and the earthworks; then turn down the road for about a third of a kilometre to pick up the footpath that returns to Kettlewell via Park Gill Beck.

Total   12½ km   8 miles

References
1. Harry Speight, *Upper Wharfedale* (Elliot Stock, 1900)
2. Ella Pontefract and Marie Hartley, *Wharfedale*, First edn (Dent, 1938).
3. Maurice Colbeck, *Yorkshire, The Dales* (Batsford, 1979)
4. Norman Duerden, *Portrait of the Dales* (Hale, 1978)
5. Arthur Raistrick, *Green Tracks on the Pennines* (Dalesman, 1962)
6. Peter Gunn, *The Yorkshire Dales. Landscape With Figures* (Century, 1984)
7. R.W. Morris, *Yorkshire Through Place Names* (David & Charles, 1982)

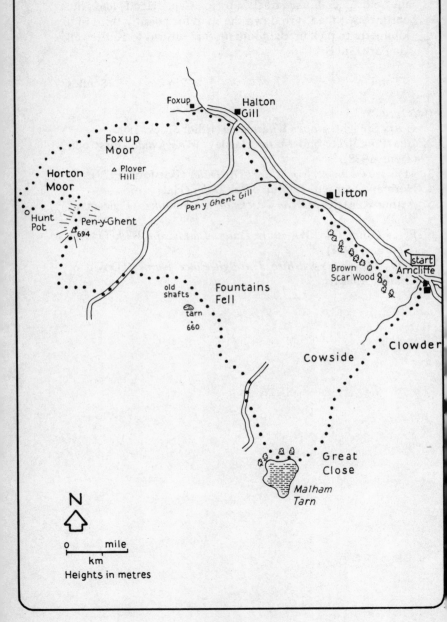

Walk 8: Fountains Fell

Arncliffe – Foxup – Pen-y-Ghent – Fountains Fell – Malham Tarn – Arncliffe

39¼ km (24½ miles) / 3,250 ft climb

SHORTER ALTERNATIVES
1. 24 km (15 miles)
2. 34¼ km (21½ miles)

O.S. 1 in 50,000, sheet 98: Wensleydale and Wharfedale area

My reason for doing this walk was because I had previously attempted to complete the Ulfkil Stride, a 33-mile walk starting and finishing in Buckden. One of the conditions of the walk is that if you take longer than five hours to reach Blishmire you are directed on a shorter route and, having failed to meet the Blishmire deadline, I wished to fill in the parts omitted on the shorter route so that on a future occasion I would be familiar with the longer route.

A suitable parking place can be found near the church in Arncliffe.

From the village green take the road that goes up the dale. Just after leaving the village the road crosses Cowside Beck then turns left to Darnbrook and Malham Tarn. At this turn take the rough stony track which runs almost parallel with the river. The stones are a nuisance underfoot, but the track is followed for only 200 yards. Bear right off the track and follow the footpath over the fields on the west bank of the river Skirfare to Litton. Do not cross the river but continue upstream to New Bridge (grid ref. 898742); then take the track to

Hesleden, cross Hesleden Beck and follow the path, still keeping to the west bank, passing Halton Gill on the other side of the river. My walk was in late April after a long dry spell. In places, the river was completely dry, and yet further upstream it was flowing freely a well-known feature of limestone country.

At Foxup the path comes out on to the road; turn left, then immediately left again off the road to Low Bergh, then after a short climb turn right for Far Bergh and Foxup Moor. It was at this point in the Ulfkil Stride that I overheard two walkers discussing the price of false teeth!

The path is well way marked. Keep Foxup Beck on your right and Plover Hill on your left, eventually crossing the watershed before passing Hull Pot, an unmistakable natural large pot-hole that confirms you are on course. The path then soon comes to the ruins of a shooting box at the junction of the lane leading down to Horton in Ribbledale (grid ref. 823743). At the shooting box turn left and follow the well-defined path up Pen-y-Ghent. From the summit take the scramble down the rocks following the Three Peaks route, but where this turns right for Horton-in-Ribblesdale keep straight ahead instead and follow the Pennine Way to Dale Head Farm and the metalled road to Halton Gill. Turn left and follow the road for 1 km to a dogs-leg bend at Blishmire (grid ref. 853723). This is the checkpoint on the Ulfkil Stride that has to be reached by 2 p.m. Failure to do so means that the competitors are directed round the shorter route of the walk. In 1984 we arrived at this point with ten minutes to spare so we were able to continue on the full route. We heard over the intercom that the winner of the full event had just finished in four hours 49 minutes.

From Blishmire turn right and follow the wall up Fountains Fell. After 200 or 300 metres the correct way is to follow the well-defined path that bears left and goes round the shoulder of Fountains Fell. The alternative route marked on the O.S. 1 in 50,000 goes straight ahead up the wallside, but this is far steeper and is not very well-defined. I have been on both paths and the one round the shoulder of Fountains Fell is the best. Follow the path to Tennant Gill and Tennant Gill Farm. Join the metalled road and watch out for the Pennine Way markers which should be followed to Malham Tarn. Turn left and follow the road past the Field Centre on the north side of the tarn.

Famous visitors to the tarn include Charles Darwin, Thomas Hughes, author of *Tom Brown's Schooldays*, John Ruskin and Charles Kingsley.[1]

For an understanding of the geology of Malham Tarn and Gordale Scar a recent publication by Derek Brumhead is worth referring to.[2]

Arthur Raistrick points out evidence of man's habitation of the Malham and Malham Moor area from earliest times:[3]

Mesolithic or Middle Stone Age: about 5,000BC.
Neolithic (New Stone Age): about 6,000BC to 3,000 BC.
Bronze Age: about 2,000BC.
Iron Age: about 300BC.
Brigantes and, contemporary with them, the Romans, recently a Roman marching camp has been found by aerial photography.
The Angles in the sixth century.
The Vikings in the ninth century.
The Danes came from the east, *The Norsemen* came from the west in the tenth and eleventh centuries.

There is little Norman influence, but the immediate area formed part of the great monastic estates of both Fountains Abbey and Bolton Priory in the twelfth and thirteenth centuries; then after the dissolution of the monasteries the estates passed into private hands.

From the field centre follow the road that goes round the north-east of Malham Tarn. At the point where the road emerges from the wood and turns south, take a compass bearing up the hill in the direction of Middle Barn (about 45°). Then, at the point where this path joins the bridle-path, turn left and follow the well-defined bridle-route past Middle House and Dew Bottoms.

Fountains Abbey had lodges on the moors with a tenant in charge and a shepherd with two or three boys as assistants to look after the flocks of sheep in summer. Middle House and Darnbrook House are examples. It was the custom to give the boys one lamb each when they started, and allow them to keep the progeny. Records are available which show that one man having received a lamb as a boy in the above way built up a flock of seventy-three ewes in the space of about twenty years.[3]

Continue on this path above Yew Cogar Scar into Arncliffe, with magnificent views of Cowside Beck on your left and Littondale ahead.

Because of the lack of pubs on this route, The Falcon at Arncliffe is all the more welcome.

Arncliffe to Blishmire	24¾ km	15½ miles
Blishmire to Arncliffe	14½ km	9 miles
Total	39¼km	24½miles

Shorter Alternatives

1. Arncliffe to New Bridge (as above) and up the track to Blishmire; then take the route from Blishmire as above, i.e. missing out Pen-y-Ghent on first section.

Arncliffe to Blishmire	9½ km	6 miles
Blishmire to Arncliffe	14½km	9 miles
Total	24 km	15 miles

2. Arnciffe to Blishmire as in the main walk, then Blishmire to New Bridge and back to Arncliffe.

Arncliffe to Blishmire	24¾km	15½ miles
Blishmire to Arncliffe	9½ km	6 miles
Total	34¼ km	21½ miles

References
1. Peter Gunn, *The Yorkshire Dales* (Century, 1984)

2. Derek Brumhead, *Geology Explained in the Yorkshire Dales and on the Yorkshire Coast* (David & Charles, 1979)
3. Arthur Raistrick, *Malham and Malham Moor* (Dalesman 1947).

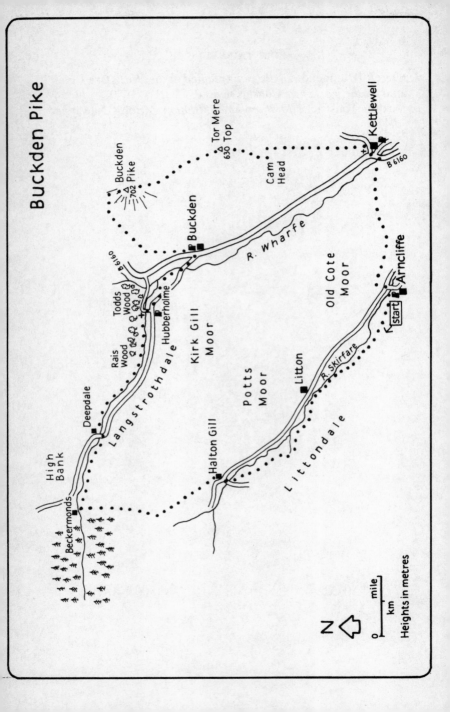

Walk 9: Buckden Pike

Arncliffe – Litton – Halton Gill – Beckermonds – Hubberholme – Buckden – Buckden Pike – Kettlewell – Arncliffe

33 km (20½ miles) / 3,540 ft climb

SHORTER ALTERNATIVES
1. 26 km (16¾ miles)
2. 23½ km (14¾ miles)

O.S. 1 in 50,000, sheet 98: Wensleydale and Wharfedale area or O.S. 1 in 25,000, Outdoor Leisure No. 30: Yorkshire Dales Northern and Central areas (note that Arncliffe is just off this map).

Park in Arncliffe, Littondale. A space can usually be found near the church.

Take the Malham road out of Arncliffe, cross Cowside Beck and take the walled stony road which runs parallel to the river. Follow the footpaths by the river upstream to Litton on the opposite side of the river to the village, then to New Bridge above Litton (grid ref. 898742), continue on the path to Hesleden and upstream to Halton Gill, where the final half kilometre into the village is on metalled road.

Halton Gill used to share a vicar with Hubberholme. This caused problems for the curate in getting from one church to the other. From 1802 to 1833 he travelled over Horse Head Moor to take the Sunday Service at Hubberhole, in later years on a white horse. When a service was due to begin at Hubberholme the locals posted a lookout and as soon as the curate was spotted the church bells were rung.

Part of a stained glass window in the church shows the vicar struggling through the snow on his horse.

Just above the village take the track to the right towards Horse Head Moor and Yockenthwaite in Wharfedale, but at the first acute bend marked on the map take the path leading 'over the top' to Beckermonds. Walk almost as far as the footbridge over Green Field Beck, then turn right and walk down-stream beside the River Wharfe. A plaque on the side of the bridge says that the footbridge was built by trainee aircrew from RAF Leeming. It is nice to know that the pilots doing their low-level training flight over the Dales are also Yorkshire Dales enthusiasts.

The walk down river by Deepdale, Yockenthwaite and then to Hubberholme is part of the Dales Way and is well waymarked. The footpath is on the opposite side of the river to the road.

Above Yockenthwaite the path passes a circle of stones which is thought to have been erected as a burial circle in the Middle Bronze Age.[1]

The origins of the name Yockenthwaite are interesting. The thirteenth-century form of the name is Yoghannesthweit which combines the Irish name Eogan with Thveit, which is Scandinavian for a clearing, thus becoming Eugan's clearing, indicating that the Vikings who settled here travelled from Norway to Ireland and in fact invaded England from the west coast.[2]

Hubberholme is just over the half-way point and a convenient stopping place for lunch. After a pint in the George Inn take the Buckden road for about 1 kilometre. Then follow the footpath by the river to the bridge at Buckden and into the village. If the full route is being followed, continue up Buckden Pike. The direct route by the waterfalls is very steep and should only be attempted by those who are used to such conditions. The more inexperienced walkers should take the footpath from the car-park through Rakes Wood, then branch off right for Buckden Pike. This diversion will add about 1½ kilometres.

From the Pike follow the boundary wall south. After about 1 kilometre a memorial cross is reached. This was erected to commemorate five Polish airmen who died when their plane crashed on 31 January 1942. There was one survivor whose life was saved by following the tracks of a fox in the snow down to Buckden. The memorial has a bronze fox's mask at its base.

Continue to follow the boundary wall in a general southerly direction and, if visibility is good enough, a reliable guide is to keep pointing in the direction of Wharfedale. On a clear day Kilnsey Crag can be seen down the valley about 5 miles away. This route now has a well-defined path. About 4½ kilomeres south of Buckden Pike the path veers torward the left (east). You are now approaching Cam Head. Magnificent views of the valley unfold whilst descending the hill into Kettlewell.

Take the main road south out of Kettlewell, cross the Wharfe turn right and follow the waymarked path for the final 2½ kilometres to Arncliffe. Conditions underfoot are very good for most of the route with very little road walking. It is mostly field paths in Littondale and again whilst following the Wharfe. The path skirting the boundary wall from Buckden Pike is soft and peaty, a delight for sore feet, as is the route from Kettlewell to Arncliffe. This is a very pleasant walk combining riverside and peaks and showing the Dales at their best.

Arncliffe to Hubberholme	17 km	10½ miles
Hubberholme to Arncliffe	16 km	10 miles
Total	33 km	20½ miles

Shorter Alternatives
First section from Arncliffe to Hubberholme as above.

17 km	10½ miles

(From Hubberholme take the above route to Buckden Bridge and, without going into Buckden, follow the riverside path on the west side of the Wharfe until you see Starbotton on the opposite bank. Go over Old Cote Moor to Arncliffe.)

	9 km	5¾ miles
Total	26 km	16¾ miles

(If the first section from Arncliffe to Hubberholme is too long this can be shortened by taking the path from Halton Gill over Horse Head Moor to Yockenthwaite and then to Hubberholme.)

Arncliffe to Hubberholme	14½km	9 miles
Hubberholme to Buckden Bridge	9 km	5¾ miles
Total	23½ km	14¾ miles

References

1. Ella Pontefract and Marie Hartley, *Wharfedale* (Dent, 1947)
2. R.W. Morris, *Yorkshire Through Place Names* (David & Charles, 1982)

Walk 10: Great Wold

Ingleton – Ingleborough – Ribble Head – Dent – High Moss – Ingleton

42¾ km (27 miles) / 4,200 ft climb

SHORTER ALTERNATIVES
1. 41 km (26½ miles)
2. 24½ km (15¼ miles)
3. 19½ km (12¾ miles)

O.S. 1 in 25,000: Outdoor Leisure
No. 2: Yorkshire Dales Western area

This is an alternative, and a contrast to the Three Peaks walk. It includes Ingleborough and part of Whernside and Gragareth. For those concerned about erosion of the footpath on the Three Peaks walk, very little of this walk is common to that of the Three Peaks. The route over Ingleborough coincides with the Three Peaks for only about half a kilometre on the summit, and again at the foot of Whernside a section of about 3 kilometres form part of that most popular of Dales walks.

Park in the public car-park in Ingleton, and follow the Hawes Road out of the village. Shortly after the junction of the Old Road to Clapham take the signposted footpath to the right up Ingleborough.

After the initial climb the path leads to a walled lane, known as Fell Lane, then follows Hard Gill for a short way. Head in an approximate north-easterly direction to the summit of Ingleborough, then follow the route of the Three Peaks off the top. After the first steep drop and about half a kilometre from the summit, leave the Three Peaks route and pick up the

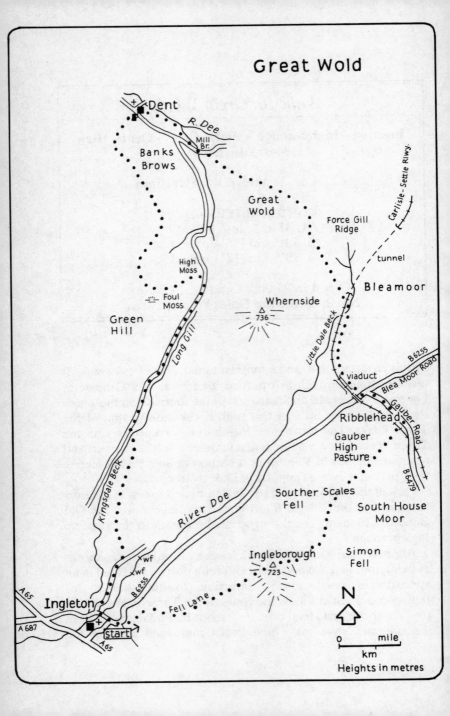

boundary wall heading north-east over the top of Simon Fell. Continue following this wall over Park Fell to New Close at grid ref. 773779. This route off Ingleborough is very easy to follow after the boundary wall has been located just below the summit of the fell. Although there is no defined footpath the walk is quite easy. From New Close follow the lane over the railway line to join the road up Ribblesdale. Here turn left and walk the 1½ kilometres to Ribble Head. At the junction of the road with the Ingleton to Hawes Road follow the footpath over Batty Green and Batty Moss to the Ribble Head viaduct. Note the warning to beware of falling masonry from the massive arches: it is advisable to keep a safe distance from the viaduct. Then, turning north and keeping the Settle to Carlisle railway line on your left, follow the route of the Three Peaks for 2 kilometres and cross the railway line at the aqueduct (grid ref. 761816). After another half kilometre a signpost points the way for the Three Peaks route up Whernside. Do not follow this but keep on the right-hand side of the fence, and follow the track over Great Wold. On the O.S. map this is marked as The Craven Way Old Road. The maximum height is about 1,770 ft. This old road is mentioned in Arthur Raistrick's *Green Tracks on the Pennines*[1] and also in Geoffrey Wright's *Roads and Trackways of the Yorkshire Dales.*[2] It is the Pack-Horse and Drover's Road from Ingleton to Dent. After reaching the highest point on this path, it soon heads roughly north-west and joins the minor road up Deepdale near Whernside Manor at grid ref. 723857. Turn right and walk to the road leading down Dentdale, then turn left and walk a quarter of a kilometre to Mill Bridge. After crossing Deepdale Beck take the footpath through the fields following Deepdale Beck and then the River Dee to Church Bridge at Dent.

Out of season the two pubs may close at 2 p.m. I was expecting them to be open until 3 p.m. so was unable to have a pub lunch. However, there are shops in Dent which sell soft drinks.

From the Church go up the village street past the granite slab which commemorates Adam Sedgwick, the native of Dent who became Woodwardian Professor at Cambridge University and

one of the founders of British geology. Walk up the cobbled
street past the Sun Inn. Round the corner is a cafe on the right
which might be useful if the pubs are closed.

Take the first road to the left leaving the village green on your
left and follow the rough track heading south-west out of Dent
up Flinter Gill. The track is covered in small stones and looks as
if it is the course of the beck when in flood. After about 1
kilometre of steady climbing you reach another track at grid ref.
698859. Turn left and follow the walled lane which follows the
contour of the hill to another 'T' junction at grid ref. 711846.
The signpost here is quite confusing, because it points right for
Whernside which is pointing towards Great Coum and
Gragareth whereas the most direct route to Whernside would
be to the left. However a close look at the map shows that this
track does change direction and eventually heads towards
Whernside, so turn right, following the walled lane heading
south-east, then south and eventually east to join the road from
Deepdale at grid ref. 724823. Turn right and follow the road
down Kingsdale for about 5 kilometres to a footbridge over
Kingsdale Beck at grid ref. 703781. Where this path joins
Twisleton Lane at grid ref. 700754 there are three alternative
routes; either straight down the road to Ingleton or follow the
footpath along the River Twiss or the River Doe back into
Ingleton. Both of the riverside paths are part of the Ingleton
waterfalls walk. There are nine waterfalls on these two stretches
of walks, and if one does this short walk (7 km) from Ingleton
there is a small charge.

Ingleton car-park to Ingleborough	5¼ km	3¼ miles
Ingleborough to Ribble Head	7 km	4¼ miles
Ribble Head to Dent	11½ km	7¼ miles
Dent to Road Junction at High Moss	8 km	5 miles
High Moss to Foot Bridge (703781)	5 km	3 miles
Foot Bridge to Ingleton	6 km	3¾ miles
Total	42¾ km	26½ miles

Shorter Alternatives

1. A slightly shorter route to Dent would be to follow the pack-horse path for most of the way. From Ingleton follow the path north alongside the River Doe past the waterfalls to Twisleton Hall. At Twisleton Lane (grid ref. 700754) take the path to the right which doubles back to Twisleton Scar End, then climb up to Ewe Top Moor and head north-east on Kirby Gate past Eller Beck, Bruntscar and Ivescar to join the route in the slightly longer walk near Turf Hill and the Ribble Head viaduct. From here follow the longer route over Great Wold to Dent.

Ingleton to Dent	22 km	13¾ miles
Same route back as in other walk	19 km	12¾ miles
Total	41 km	26½ miles

2. Route as in the main walk from Ingleton to Ingleborough and Ribble Head (12¼ km) 7¾ miles.

    From the Station Inn at Ribble Head take the path heading north-west keeping the viaduct on your left. Cross under the railway line by the bridge at grid ref. 757804 just north of Turf Hill. Thus you will avoid going under the Ribble Head viaduct which is in a dangerous state. Follow the old pack-horse route back to Ingleton via Ivescar, Brunscar, Kirby Gate and Ewes Top Moss and Twisleton Lane where there are three alternatives back to Ingleton, (a) down the road, (b) follow the path along the River Twiss, or (c) that along the River Doe.

	12¼ km	7¾ miles
	12 km	7½ miles
Total	24¼ km	15¼ miles

3. Route as in the main walk from Ingleton to Ingleborough (5¼ km) 3¼ miles.

Take the path heading south off Ingleborough. After just over 1 kilometre there is a fork in the path. Take the left-hand fork heading south-east towards Gaping Gill. If visibility is good enough the pot-hole can be seen from about 600 feet above on the flanks of Ingleborough. The main shaft of Gaping Hill is 340 feet deep. The fascinating story of the history of Gaping Gill and Ingleborough Cave, from the first descent of the main shaft by Edward Martel in 1895 to the long-awaited confirmation of the link between Gaping Gill and Ingleborough Cave in 1983, is told in *Gaping Gill: 150 Years of Exploration* by Howard M. Beck.[3] This book is recommended to anyone visiting the area whether as a pot-holer or not, because much of the pioneering work in underground exploration has been carried out in the Dales, and the Gaping Gill complex is Britain's most celebrated cave system. However, it must be stressed that novices should not enter pot-holes unless accompanied by an expert and wearing the appropriate clothing. In the past, pot-holing clubs have run a service to the general public lowering them down into the main chamber of Gaping Gill. There is no charge for going down, but you have to pay to be hauled back to the surface again!

From Gaping Gill follow the path south down the impressive limestone gorge of Trow Gill to the mouth of Ingleborough Cave.

Guided tours of the cave are available daily apart from mid-January to mid-February. If you intend to go on one of these underground tours remember to wear warm clothing, because the temperature underground is almost constant throughout the year and a great contrast with the outside temperature in summer.

Walk down into Clapham, then follow the paths back to Ingleton between the old and new road, for example along Laithbutts Lane to Newby, Goat Gap, Cold Cotes Waste, Greenwood Leghe, then by footpath back into Ingleton.

Ingleton to Ingleborough	5¼ km	3¾ miles
Ingleborough to Clapham	6¾ km	4¼ miles
Clapham to Ingleton	7½ km	4¾ miles
Total	19½ km	12¾ miles

References
1. Arthur Raistrick, *Green Tracks on the Pennines* (Dalesman, 1962)
2. Geoffrey N. Wright, *Roads and Trackways of the Yorkshire Dales* (Moorland, 1985)
3. Howard M. Beck, *Gaping Gill: 150 Years of Exploration* (Hale, 1984).

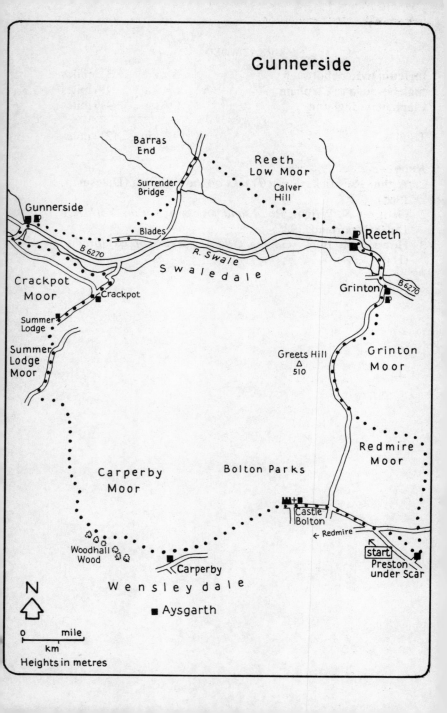

Walk 11: Gunnerside

Preston-under-Scar – Castle Bolton – Carperby Pasture – Summer Lodge – Gunnerside – Blades – Reeth – Grinton – Preston

45½ km (28¾ miles) / 1,600 ft climb

SHORTER ALTERNATIVES
1. 30½ km (19¼ miles)
2. 23 km (14½ miles)

O.S. 1 in 50,000, sheet 98: Wensleydale and Wharfedale area, O.S. 1 in 50,000, sheet 92: Barnard Castle and Richmond area O.S. 1 in 50,000,sheet 99: Northallerton and Ripon area (very little of the route is on this map). The major part of the walk is on sheet 98 or O.S. 1 in 25,000; Outdoor Leisure No. 30: Northern and Central areas.

Preston-under-Scar is a farming village about 3 miles west of Leyburn in Wensleydale.

From Leyburn travel by car up Wensleydale towards Hawes. At Wensley turn right and Preston-under-Scar is off the main road before you reach Redmire. Park in the village.

Preston-under-Scar was the home of many of the lead-miners working at Keld Heads Mine to the east of the village and Cobscar Smelt Mill on Preston Moor. Keld Heads Mine is the oldest in Wensleydale for which there is a record and is known to have been worked in the twelfth century.[2] It was the richest lead-mine in the county. At the height of its working life it employed 250 men and boys. The effluent from the lead smelt mills was condensed in long flues running up the hillside behind the mill. This served two purposes: to prevent pollution and to recover the condensate. A water-cooled condenser was built 550 feet above Keld Heads Smelt Mill. Its efficiency can be judged by the production for the year following June 1856, when 1,374 tons of ore were smelted and 96 tons 13 cwt of lead were extracted as fume. The flue was extended in 1855 to a total length of nearly two miles, ending in a square stack near Cobscar Mill. Keld Heads Mine closed at the end of the nineteenth century, due to the flooding of the lowest levels of the mine by the river Ure, thus making the ore harder to mine, and also because of the falling price of smelted lead.

Walk west on the road through Preston-under-Scar. At the end of the village you will pass some new bungalows on your right. Go through a gate also on your right, follow the fence which goes past a solitary house which belonged to a gamekeeper until about 1980. The track is replaced by a path going through the woods. The path comes out on the Redmire to Richmond road at Scarth Nick. Turn left and walk down the road for 200 metres or so to the junction of the road from Leyburn at grid ref. 057916 sheet 98. At this junction leave the road and take the metalled farm track following the contour of the hill to the west. After 1½ kilometres this track comes to the Redmire to Grinton road. Cross and follow the road into Castle Bolton. The castle was built by Richard, Lord Scrope, who began building works in 1379 when he was Lord Chancellor of England. It took eighteen years to complete at a cost of £12,000.[1] Most of the timber came from the forest of Engleby in Cumberland, and was conveyed to Bolton by oxen.

Mary Queen of Scots was imprisoned here from 13 July 1568 to 26 January 1569. Her retinue totalled forty, half of whom had to be billeted in the village. Sir George Bowes of Barnard Castle (now Bowes museum) supplied hangings and extra bedding from his own house for the Queen's visit.[3] A local legend suggests that the Queen escaped from the castle and was re-captured on Leyburn Shawl at Queen's Gap.[4] This legend is so strong that the local authority have erected a sign at Queen's Gap to this effect but the legend cannot be substantiated. A more likely reason for Mary Queen of Scots being moved on from Castle Bolton was the visit of Lady Scrope's brother, the Duke of Norfolk who proposed marriage to the captive Queen, and as the Duke was the head of the Catholic Church in England, this was more than Queen Elizabeth could tolerate and it led to the Duke's arrest and eventual execution.[1]

During the Civil Wars the castle was held by the Richmondshire Cavaliers fighting for the King. They were besieged by the forces of Cromwell and had to live on horse flesh. Today the castle is open to the public and a meal can be obtained in the main dining room with the slogan 'Dine where a Queen once dined'.

Walk through the village on the road between castle and church, then follow the track over Bolton Parks to its junction with Beldon Beck. Turn left going south to intersect the minor road above Carperby and follow the green track that crosses New Pasture parallel to the minor road through Carperby. This track goes past some old lead-mine workings below Ivy Scar, then turns north-west. Head towards a shooting box on the skyline at Woodhall Greets. At the shooting box try to follow the path that intersects the Askrigg to Low Row road at the Fleak (grid ref. 964941) but it will be necessary to take a compass bearing at the shooting box because the path is poorly defined: this requires walking on rough heather for 1 to 2 kilometres.

On reaching the road turn right (north) and after 1 kilometre at grid ref. 964948 where the road bends to the east, take the well-defined track to the left that drops down to Summer Lodge, then walk 2 kilometres down the road to Crackpot. At the junction in Crackpot either turn left and go along the road to Gunnerside, or alternatively turn right, then at grid ref. 975972 turn left and take the riverside track to Gunnerside.

The King's Head at Gunnerside is a convenient stopping place for lunch, but an early morning start will be necessary to get to the pub before closing time.

The name Gunnerside is derived from the Norse personal name Gunnarr and Saetr: that is Gunnar's upland pasture.[5]

During the eighteenth and nineteenth centuries most of the inhabitants of Gunnerside were lead-miners who worked in one of the many lead-mines in Gunnerside Gill which runs for 5 kilometres north of the village. They walked the long distance every day to their mine or smelt mill, often knitting as they walked.[2]

From Gunnerside, take the B6270 road east and at the top of the village fork left, near a tap set into the wall. At the next junction turn right, this track eventually becomes a green lane, follow this to Blades. Turn left in this little hamlet at grid ref. 980984. Walk north, then north-east, to join the road at Surrender Bridge (not named on the map) at grid ref. 989999, sheet 98. Walk north up the road for 1 kilometre to the water-splash at Barras End (grid ref. 993010 sheet 92). Cross the water-splash and turn right, following the bridle-path going south-east until it emerges at Riddings (grid ref. 028996 sheet 98). Then walk down the road to Reeth and across the fields to Grinton. If you are on time have a couple of pints at the Bridge Inn.

A visit to the church to see the magnificent carved oak canopy above the font is also worthwhile.

From the Bridge Inn take the minor road going south towards Redmire and after 1 kilometre take the left-hand fork past Grinton Lodge Youth Hostel. After 1 kilometre cross the bridge over Cogden Gill, leave the road and follow Cogden Gill up to Grinton Smelt Mill. This is the best-preserved relic of the lead-mining industry in the Dales. It has been preserved because of its use for local farming needs. The smelt mill is described in Clough[2] as well as in Arthur Raistrick's book.[6] The present building was probably erected in 1820-22. Arthur Raistrick deduced that this was the re-buiding period from the fact that, although Grinton mines produced lead during this period, none of it was smelted at Grinton.

A close examination of the mortar in the flue will show little black flecks. This is the waste from the lead smelting. It is lead oxide and is a sure indication of the abundance of lead at the time that the flue was built. In less affluent times the lead oxide would have been re-melted in order to extract as much lead as possible.

Another interesting feature is the fact that the flue was directed through the peat store so that the heat from the waste gases could be used to dry out the peat.

Follow the gill south-west up to the right from the smelt mill. This can be climbed with ease to the point where the stream crosses the Grinton to Redmire road; then turn left and follow this road for 2½ kilometres over the brow of the hill. Leave the road at grid ref. 046935, sheet 98 and follow the un-metalled track to the site of Cobscar Smelt Mill (grid ref. 059930), then on O.S. sheet 99 follow the track downhill to cross the Redmire to Richmond road and the final mile into Preston-under-Scar.

Preston-under-Scar to Gunnerside	22 km	13¾ miles
Gunnerside to Preston-under-Scar	23½ km	15 miles
Total	45½ km	28¾ miles

Shorter Alternatives
1. Park in Castle Bolton. Take the same route as in the walk above through Bolton Parks to Beldon Beck; then follow the path that eventually comes out near the Fleak at grid ref. 964941 and, still following north on the Askrigg to Low Row road, instead of leaving the road for Summer Lodge continue for another 3 kilometres to Birks End at grid ref. 986968. Turn left and follow the path downhill to join the track by the river Swale at grid ref. 983974.

   From here the riverside tracks can be followed on the south side of the Swale in an easterly direction to Grinton.

   From Grinton follow the road going south for 1 kilometre to Grinton Lodge Youth Hostel and 1 kilometre beyond the hostel leave the road at the bridge over Cogden Gill to follow the Gill in a southerly direction to Grinton Smelt Mill. Strike off right at this point, still following the gill which crosses the Redmire to Grinton Road at grid ref. 038963, then follow the path which is signposted to Greets

Hill and turn south onto the path crossing Apedale to Castle Bolton.

Castle Bolton to Grinton	22½ km	14¼ miles
Grinton to Castle Bolton	8 km	5 miles
Total	30½ km	19¼ miles

2. Starting in Castle Bolton follow the same route as above to The Fleak at grid ref. 964941 and continue on the minor road to grid ref. 983964. Turn south-west to cross Whitaside Moor on the path that goes down Apedale and at the shooting hut (grid ref. 031942) turn south to follow the path back to Castle Bolton.

Total	23 km	14½ miles

References

1. Harry Speight, *Romantic Richmondshire* (Elliot Stock 1897)
2. Robert Clough, *The Lead Smelting Mills of the Yorkshire Dales and Northern Pennines*, Second edn. (Clough, 1980)
3. Ella Pontefract, *Wensleydale* (Dent, 1936)
4. Halliwell Sutcliffe, *The Striding Dales* (Fredericke Warne, 1929)
5. R.W. Morris, *Yorkshire Through Place Names* (David & Charles, 1982)
6. Arthur Raistrick, *The Lead Industry of Wensleydale and Swaledale*, Volume 2: *The Smelting Mills* (Moorland, 1975)

Walk 12: Marsett Bridge

Castle Bolton – Carperby – Thoralby – Marsett – Hawes – Newbiggin – Castle Bolton

44½ km (28 miles) / 3,000 ft climb

SHORTER ALTERNATIVE
21 km (13½ miles)

O.S. 1 in 50,000, sheet 98: Wensleydale and Wharfedale area or O.S. 1 in 25,000, Outdoor Leisure No. 30: Yorkshire Dales, Northern and Central areas

From the Dales car-park at Castle Bolton walk west away from the castle. Beyond the first small patch of trees follow the waymarked path heading south-west to West Bolton and Carperby. In spite of the waymarks I found it necessary to consult the map occasionally. The path joins the road at East End Farm in Carperby. Walk one third of a kilometre into the village to the Wheatsheaf. Opposite the pub, follow the footpath heading south-east then south to Aysgarth. Cross the Yore Bridge and walk up the road to its junction with the A684. Turn right and immediately leave the road by a path heading south-west to Tomgill Bridge at grid ref. 005875. Walk down the road into Thoralby. Walk west through the village, then take one of the tracks heading west-south-west. It doesn't matter which because the two tracks converge at a gate at Brown-a-How (grid ref. 967978). From here follow the track, still heading west-south-west to intersect Busk Lane at grid ref. 937847. *Note*: this section of path from Brown-a-How to Busk Lane is very poorly defined (I lost it!) and I found it necessary

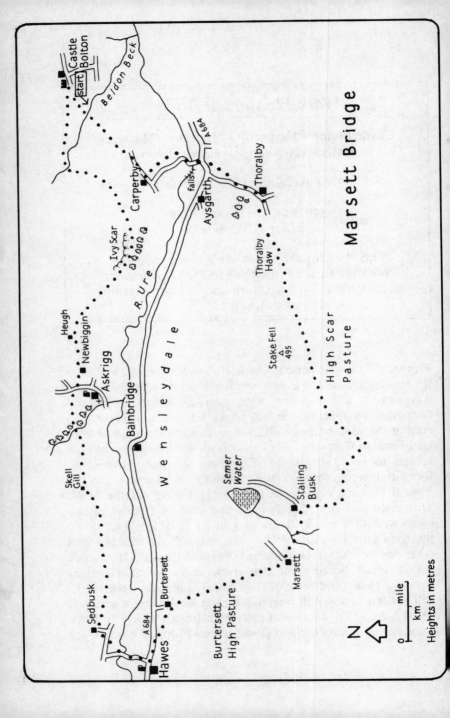

to walk on a compass bearing. This inevitably slows one down.

From the intersection of Busk Lane at grid ref. 937847 turn left and walk two-thirds of a kilometre to grid ref. 935840 where the track from Kidstones to Stalling Busk is reached. Turn right and walk into Stalling Busk, then follow the walled lane down to Raydale, Marsett Beck and Marsett. *Note that this section is prone to flooding and after prolonged rainfall it might be impassable*, or, at the least, be prepared for a pair of wet feet.

(The BBC were filming the James Herriot television series at Marsett Bridge the day I did this walk.)

Cross the bridge and turn left, heading west. After a quarter of a kilometre turn right to follow the path heading north-west to the Roman road and cross to the east of Wether Fell at grid ref. 895877; then follow the path north to Burtersett. This joins with the road at the south-east corner of the village. Head north out of the village. On the outskirts look for a stile on the left and take the field path to Hawes.

Follow the minor road heading north out of Hawes towards Hardraw and the Buttertubs. Immediately after crossing the River Ure follow the footpath heading north-east over the fields to Sedbusk. Before you come to the village take the field road heading east; this passes to the south of a farm at Litherskew. Still walking east and roughly parallel with the road, pass Shaw Cote at grid ref. 911910; shortly afterwards the path turns north-east to enter Skell Gill. Walk 1½ kilometres east along Skell Gill Lane and at a right-angle in the lane take the footpath heading north-east to join Low Straits Lane at grid ref. 942918. Follow this lane east for three-quarters of a kilometre to the minor road, turn right towards Askrigg and, after a quarter of a kilometre turn left onto the field path to Newbiggin. Continue on the field path heading east-north-east through a small wood to join a better-defined path at Heugh (grid ref. 962917). Follow this path south-east to a point north of Woodhall at grid ref. 978906, then join the Oxclose Road heading east through New Pasture. This path is on soft turf – a bonus for sore feet. The path turns north to cross a ford at grid ref. 009918. Follow the path east for 2 kilometres to Castle Bolton.

Castle Bolton to Hawes	25 km	15½ miles
Hawes to Castle Bolton	19½ km	12½ miles
Total	44½ km	28 miles

Shorter Alternative

Follow the main walk from Castle Bolton via West Bolton and Carperby to Aysgarth. From Yore Bridge walk up to the A684 and turn left. After about 100 metres take the footpath on the right leading to Eshington Bridge at grid ref. 014877. Cross the bridge and immediately follow a footpath on the right heading south then south-east to West Burton. From the village follow the farm track past Flanders Hall (grid ref. 020872). Continue on this track to its junction with a minor road at grid ref. 062877. Walk down the road for 1 kilometre to West Witton. Alternatively, from West Burton take the path at the north end of the village green which leads to the bridge over Walden Beck. Follow the path heading east up Penhill and continue due east to the plateau on the top of Penhill. From the trig point follow the path east to join the minor road and walk down to West Witton.

On the main road in West Witton at grid ref. 063884 take the track heading north-east to Lord's Bridge at grid ref. 075893, then follow the path heading north-west to Redmire. Here a path leads to Castle Bolton.

Castle Bolton to Aysgarth to West Burton	7 km	4½ miles
West Burton to West Witton	7 km	4½ miles
West Witton to Castle Bolton	7 km	4½ miles
Total	21 km	13½ miles

West Burton – Buckden Pike – Buckden – Starbotton – Coverdale – West Burton

37 km (23 miles) / 3,300 ft climb

SHORTER ALTERNATIVE
22 km (13¾ miles)

O.S. 1 in 50,000, sheet 98: Wensleydale and Wharfedale area, or O.S. 1 in 25,000: Outdoor Leisure No. 30: Yorkshire Dales Northern and Central areas

Park in West Burton. Walk south through the village from the village green. Take the right-hand fork in the road past a modern house on your right, and follow a footpath over styles to Newbiggin. Go straight through the village, then follow the track leading up the hill and out of Newbiggin. The track eventually peters out on Noughtberry hill, but if you are in doubt about the direction, go upwards, then keep parallel with the road up Bishopdale. Noughtberry Hill is named after the mountain fruit growing on it: the noughtberry which is a local name for the cloudberry. It is a red fruit when ripe, rather like a raspberry, but the plant and its leaf are similar to the strawberry. The fruits ripen in early July and can be eaten raw, although they are full of seeds. The locals in Newbiggin make jam out of them. There are several acres of the fruit up here. I have never seen them before. However, there are two other peaks with similar spellings in the district, Great Knoutberry Hill on Widdale Fell and Knoutberry Haw on Bough Fell.

Keeping parallel with Bishopdale continue to climb until you

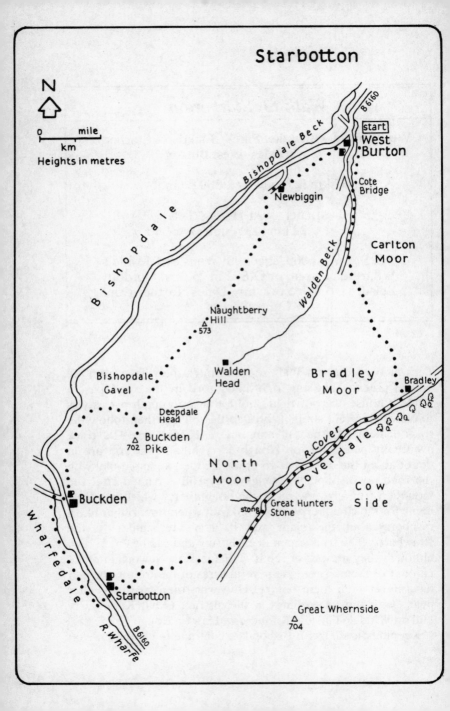

see a line of shooting butts ahead. Where there are shooting butts there is always a path between them. Follow the butts to a wall where a path follows up the wall to the trig point on top of Buckden Pike. Cross the wall to the trig point. This is one of my particular favourite peaks and I have approached it from all possible directions, in all types of weather, from the hot summer day when there is not a breath of air, even at this height, and butterflies have been on the top of the Pike – to the other extreme on a New Year's Day approaching from Walden Head when we were walking on snow and ice all the time and never saw a patch of grass, on reaching the summit it was so cold that we felt hyperthermia setting in almost immediately. It is natural to want a rest after reaching the summit but even in summer a stop on the tops is often regretted later because the cooling wind can very easily bring on cramp. I have learned, the hard way, to quickly admire the view and descend to a more sheltered spot before stopping.

From the trig point double back for 200 to 300 yards to join a path following down another wall at right angles to the first wall. This path leads to Cray but on the flat ground above Cray pick up the waymarked path to the left which leads to Buckden car-park.

My time from West Burton to Buckden (10 miles) was just 3 hours. So with careful planning it was possible to get a quick pint at The Buck then on to Starbotton for another pint before 3 p.m.

From Buckden follow the road towards Hubberholme and immediately over the river at Buckden Bridge take the waymarked path to the left which follows the river Wharfe downstream. At Starbotton cross the river again, by either stepping stones or footbridge, to go back into the village.

Starbotton is the half-way point, 18½ km and so well worth another pint at the Fox and Hounds. Two pubs slowed me down considerably – the last mile-and-a-half 2½ km taking two hours. (I saw a tree-creeper in a beech tree by the Wharfe.)

From Starbotton take the rough road behind the pub towards Cam Head. The track is well-defined up to the boundary wall.

On this track you pass old lead-mine waste heaps and the remains of an old Bayle Hill, a primitive smelt mill; facing the prevailing wind, it was used for lead smelting before the use of water power to drive the bellows.

Immediately past the boundary wall turn right and follow the wall side past the earthwork marked on the O.S. 1 in 50,000 map. These earthworks are thought to have been built by the Brigantes to prevent the Roman soldiers from using the main routes to the north. The wall ends about half a mile before joining the road in Coverdale, and it is necessary to strike off in a north-easterly direction to intersect the road.

My last half hour was not as solitary as I would have expected. I thought I was entirely alone until the silence was suddenly broken by a fell runner coming up behind me. Other signs of human activity were a hang-glider stationary half way up Great Whernside, and soon another hang-glider took off from the same ridge. He glided for two or three minutes and landed a few hundred yards short of the Coverdale road which I knew lay ahead of me but which was still out of sight.

For the last half mile or so there is no path but the ground is not too uneven underfoot. On reaching the road turn left and walk down Coverdale to Bradley, about 5 kilometres, then take the path over Carlton Moor to Walden Dale. Follow the path out of the village and head up the hillside to the left by the side of a stream.

Take a compass bearing for the point in Walden Dale where the path joins the road at grid ref. 017838. It is all too easy to rely on your sense of direction and then to get lost, so use the compass instead, as it is far more reliable. When the road in Walden Dale is reached turn right and follow the road to West Burton.

West Burton to Starbotton	18½ km	11½ miles
Starbotton to West Burton	18½ km	11½ miles
Total	37 km	23 miles

Shorter Alternative

Follow the route as above to the trig point on Buckden Pike, then walk east for half a kilometre to intersect the path heading north-east. Then follow the stream to Walden Head and Kentucky Farm. From here there are alternative routes back to West Burton on both sides of Walden Beck either by road or road and path. The latter is preferable as the road alone is rather dull.

Total about 13¾ miles (22 km) depending on the route taken.

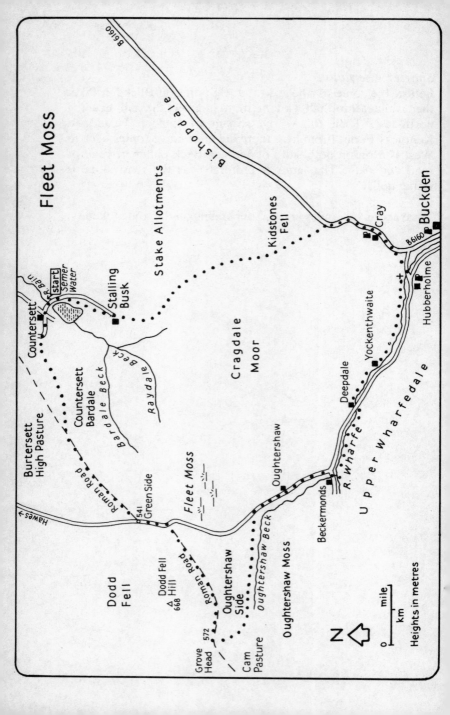

Walk 14: Fleet Moss

Semer Water – Roman Road – Oughtershaw Beck – Beckermonds – Hubberholme – Cray – Kidstones – Stalling Busk – Semer Water

37 km (23 miles) / 2,150 ft climb

SHORTER ALTERNATIVE
19½ km (12¼ miles)

O.S. 1 in 50,000, sheet 98: Wensleydale and Wharfedale area, or O.S. 1 in 25,000, Outdoor Leisure No. 30: Yorkshire Dales Northern and Central areas

Park on the north side of Semer Water. The path you will follow can be seen from the lake if you look west. It climbs Wether Fell from the Burtersett Road. Follow the road from the lake across the River Bain towards Countersett. At the top of the first steep hill take the second turn on the left up the road towards Burtersett. Down the hill on your right is Countersett Hall. This was once the home of Richard Robinson, the first Quaker in Wensleydale.[1] He was born at Preston-under-Scar in 1628. It was due to his influence that Quakerism was particularly strong in Raydale. For this reason there is no pub in the dale.

Continue along the road going towards Burtersett. At a sharp right-hand bend in the road (grid ref. 912878) go through the gate on the left into the field beyond and follow the path which goes in a south-westerly direction towards Wether Fell. The path skirts the front of the hill, then follows open moorland until it joins the Roman road near Wether Fell. The steepness of the climb from the lake is guaranteed to get your heart pumping and the sweat flowing freely, but you are well rewarded by the views of the lake and, later, the easy walking on the springy turf.

The 'sett' ending of place names in the district (e.g. Countersett, Burtersett, Marsett and Appersett above Hawes) is evidence of a Viking settlement in the district.[2] The Norse word 'Saetr' applied to the upland pasture and to the huts which the shepherds and the cattle herdsmen used in the summer months.

Wether Fell derives its name from the grazing place of the wethers. (A wether is a castrated ram.) Another example of a place-name containing wether is Wetherby, 'by' being the old Scandinavian for a farm: hence 'the farm where the wethers are kept'.

When you reach the Roman road follow it in a south-westerly direction past the hang-gliding club to the junction of the Hawes to Buckden road on Fleet Moss. Turn left and follow this road for about three quarters of a kilometre; then at a left turn in the road follow the Roman road again which at this point is tarmac covered.

This Roman road can be traced from Bainbridge over Fleet Moss and for a distance of about 20 miles in the direction of Ingleton and towards Lancaster. Its course can be seen on the O.S. map.

This section of the Roman road is followed for about 3 kilometres until it joins the Pennine Way at grid ref. 829834. At this point take the path heading south (difficult to locate) which, after about 1 kilometre joins the Dales Way route at the watershed between Oughtershaw Beck and Cam Beck (grid ref. 834823). This is the watershed of England. At this point water may travel west by Cam Beck and the River Ribble to Morecambe Bay and the Irish Sea or if it falls only a few feet to the east its destination may be the North Sea, by way of Oughtershaw Beck, the River Wharfe and later the Ouse to join the Humber.

At the watershed turn left (east) and follow the Dales Way path by the side of Oughtershaw Beck to Swarthgill, then follow the farm track to Oughtershaw where you continue along the metalled road for 1½ kilometres, before turning right to Beckermonds.

Go into the village then turn left and cross the footbridge over Green Field Beck. Turn left again and walk downstream.

The junction of Greenfield Beck and Oughtershaw Beck is the start of the River Wharfe.

Follow the Dales Way, from Beckermonds to Hubberholme, which is waymarked, keeping on the opposite side of the river to the road, and cross the river at Deepdale. Hubberholme is a convenient place for lunch and a couple of pints at the George Inn, followed by a quick look at the Rood Loft in the church. Very few of these structures are extant. As they were made of wood, they were easy to destroy in the time of the Dissolution of the Monasteries. This one probably survived because of the remoteness of its location The date 1558 is carved on it in Roman numerals, the year in which Elizabeth I became Queen.

Whilst we were in the church we heard about the fire that had destroyed part of York Minster the previous night. Two Australian girls who were looking round the church at the time were particularly upset on hearing the news because they had visited York Minster only the day before.

Take the Cray road out of Hubberholme, and after 1 kilometre, just before the first road junction, follow the footpath at the side of Cray Gill. You will pass some delightful little waterfalls, but before you reach the last and biggest fall, strike uphill to the left to a gate which leads into Cray. Here there is another chance of a drink at the White Lion, opening hours permitting.

I have heard a tale about farmers meeting in the White Lion on their way back to Wensleydale from the Kilnsey Show. One says to the other 'Hast tha' got thi tup with thee?' The answer was obviously 'yes', because the first farmer then said 'Fetch 'im in'. Then followed a lively evening in the pub, the main attraction being a prize tup (ram) from the Kilnsey Show.

Take the metalled road from Cray uphill for 1½ kilometres to the top of Kidstones Pass and at grid ref. 943084 follow the track on the left leading over Stake Moss and eventually down to Stalling Busk. This is a very pleasant track 'over the tops'.

When walking on such a track one tends to wonder about its origins. Why is such a well-defined track apparently going nowhere of any importance? That might be so today, but in the days when it was built its importance was more obvious. It is in fact part of the Roman road from Ilkley to the Roman fort at Bainbridge. Geoffrey Wright describes the section of this road between Bainbridge and Buckden.[3] The Roman road mainly followed the course of the present modern metalled road going in a general southerly direction from Bainbridge to a point just to the east of Stalling Busk. It then headed south on the present minor road to a point near Bank Wood where it followed the course of the path joining the minor road again at grid ref. 933833, then again followed the course of the modern road to Cray High Bridge at grid ref. 944797. From here it followed the footpath on the O.S. map through Rakes Wood to the car-park at Buckden. This section of the old Roman road is locally known as Lady Anne's Way. Lady Anne Clifford used this track on her journey north from her castle at Skipton when going to Pendragon Castle.

Walking down from Stake Moss towards Stalling Busk we saw a group of figures coming down the hill from Fairy Haw towards the track in front of us. There were at least ten people. At first it appeared to be a mountain rescue team, but on getting closer it turned out to be the army on manoeuvres. There were two teams of soldiers, two or three per team walking in line with harnesses around their shoulders supporting tree trunks on either side of them. They stopped at a check-point on the road for refreshments, then carried on to Bank Wood.

Walk down into Stalling Busk, then to Raydale Beck and along the south-east side of Semer Water back to the car.

Semer Water to Hubberholme	24 km	15 miles
Hubberholme to Semer Water	13 km	8 miles
Total	37 km	23 miles

Shorter Alternative

Park in Burtersett. Follow the footpaths over the fields to Hawes, then follow the Pennine Way south to its junction with the Roman road at grid ref. 829834, turn left and follow the Roman road to its junction with the Hawes to Hubberholme road at grid ref. 861846. Turn left then right after three-quarters of a kilometre and continue following the Roman road towards Bainbridge. Leave this track at grid ref. 882870 to follow the footpath over Wether Fell to Burtersett.

Total   19½ km   12¼ miles

This shorter walk does not have a pub half-way for a break for lunch, but all is not lost. It is possible as an alternative to park the car just off the Fleet Moss road at the start of either section of the Roman road and to do the same walk from a different starting-point. This will mean that Hawes can be used as the midday break point with its selection of pubs and eating places.

References

1. Ella Pontefract, *Wensleydale*, First edn (Dent, 1936)
2. R.W.Morris, *Yorkshire Through Place Names* (David & Charles, 1982)
3. Geoffrey N. Wright, *Roads and Trackways of the Yorkshire Dales* (Moorland, 1985).

Semer Water

Askrigg
Skell Gill
Coleby Hall
Bainbridge
Start
A 684
R. Bain
Sedbusk
Hawes
A 684
B 6255
Gayle
Ten End
△ 584
Duerley Beck
Pennine Way
Dodd
Fell Hill
△ 668
Roman Road
Bardale Head
Bardale Beck
Marsett
Semer Water
Stalling Busk
Raydale Beck

N

0   km   mile

Heights in metres

Walk 15: Semer Water

**Bainbridge – Semer Water – Marsett – Bardale Head –
Roman Road – Pennine Way – Hawes – Sedbusk –
Askrigg – Bainbridge**

35km (22 miles) / 1,350 ft climb
SHORTER ALTERNATIVE
21 km (13¼ miles)

O.S. 1 in 50,000, sheet 98: Wensleydale and
Wharfedale area, or all but the smallest section of
this walk is on the O.S. 1 in 25,000, Outdoor Leisure
No 30: Yorkshire Dales Northern and Central
areas.

The land on the south side of Semer Water is prone to flooding, making it difficult to cross Raydale Beck. This walk should therefore not be attempted after long spells of heavy rain. Even in dry weather, a ford over Raydale Beck has to be crossed, so it is advisable to carry a towel and take off your boots before crossing the beck. Alternatively, I found that trainers were ideal footwear, because they could be worn when crossing the beck, so avoiding damage to the feet, and the water was quickly squeezed out of the shoes by the continuous flexing action of walking.

The River Bain, which flows out of Semer Water to join the River Ure at Bainbridge, is the shortest river in England, being just over 2 miles long, but to see it in full spate after heavy rain is a wonderful sight and fully justifies its claim to be a river and not a stream.

Just to the east of Bainbridge village is a flat-topped hillock called Brough Hill. It has a Roman fort on its summit. This has not been extensively excavated, probably because the site is a long way from any large towns. However, a trial trench was dug there in 1925[1] and from this excavation there is evidence that the site was probably occupied for the major part of the Roman period, and that, like other forts in Yorkshire, it was frequently rebuilt. Evidence also suggests that the first fortifications were built on this site at the end of the first century AD and may have been supervised by Agricola. Apparently the fort was stormed by the Brigantes in the rebellion of AD 115 and subsequently rebuilt. The earliest buildings here were earthworks together with walls of timber, and at a later rebuilding these were replaced by stone buildings. Stone from the Roman camp must have been used to build the present village of Bainbridge. The fort was certainly inhabited at the beginning of the fourth century and pottery discovered on the site suggests that it was occupied until the end of the Roman period.

Another place of historical interest in Bainbridge is the pub, the Rose and Crown. Above the door of the pub at one time was a stone bearing the date 1445, although this must have been transferred from another building, as the porch itself is of a later date.[2] It is interesting to note that the symbol of the 'Rose and Crown' was depicted on one of the badges of the House of Lancaster.

There are some stocks on the village green. According to Spate[2] they were last used to punish a tinker and his wife for being drunk and disorderly.

There are plenty of suitable places to park the car in Bainbridge. Walk out of the village on the main road towards Aysgarth. Just before the minor road heading south to Stalling Busk, there is a signpost pointing across a field to Semer Water. Follow this path to the bridge over the river Bain at the north end of the lake, turn left and walk half a kilometre to Low Blean Farm where after crossing a second stream, a signpost and stile on the right point the way to Stalling Busk. This is a very pleasant walk by the side of the lake.

There is a legend about the origin of Semer Water in which

an angel came to Stalling Busk disguised as a beggar. On being turned away from all the houses he put a curse on the village and the waters of the lake rose and flooded the village.

I prefer the geological explanation of the lake's origin: it is both more feasible and more fascinating. During the Ice Age a glacier was gouging its way down Wensleydale, thus blocking the way of a second glacier coming down Raydale. When the ice melted, the rubble that had been pushed in front of the glacier formed a terminal moraine behind which water collected in the form of a large lake. Eventually the lake burst its banks and formed the course of the present river Bain. Due to continual erosion the river bed has become deeper and thus lowered the level of the lake.

The large stone at the north end of the lake, the Carlow Stone, was carried by the glacier from greater altitudes. Turner, the landscape painter, drew a view of Semer Water from the Carlow Stone. This picture was used as the frontispiece for the most expensive edition of Speight's book.

It is likely that primitive man may have lived on the shores of Semer Water in pile dwellings. Piles were driven into the bed of the lake and huts supported on a platform above the water. No evidence of these piles has been found, but the level of the lake was lowered in 1937 for land reclaimation and shortly afterwards a Bronze Age spearhead was discovered on the shores of the lake.[3]

Semer Water is noted for the variety of birds that visit its shores. Today, water sports are allowed on the lake in the summer months but are banned in winter so as not to disturb the migrating birds.

Continue on the path along the east side of the lake. Close to Stalling Busk the path passes the ruins of a church. This church was built in 1603 and served Stalling Busk and Marsett nearby as it had no church of its own. It fell into ruin during the Civil War and was rebuilt in 1722. Stalling Busk now has another church.[4]

From the church take the right-hand path which joins the lane leading from Stalling Busk to Marsett. Turn right at the lane, cross Cragdale Water and the ford over Raydale Beck and walk up the lane to Marsett. Cross over the bridge at Bardale Beck, then immediately turn left to follow the path marked on the O.S. map which goes alongside Bardale Beck. This is a very quiet and secluded stretch of the walk and one of those places which gives you a sense of achievement for having found it, especially if you are walking on your own. The path eventually leaves the beck and climbs up the hillside to the open moors, and finally reaches the road over Fleet Moss at grid ref. 862846 in the middle of a section of double bends on the road. On reaching the road turn right and after about 200 metres turn left to follow the Roman Road (now metalled) 3½ kilometres to the west. Turn right at grid ref. 830834 and follow the Pennine Way northward to Hawes. This section is well-marked and therefore no further directions are necessary.

Hawes contains sufficient variation in eating and drinking places to cater for all tastes. Bar lunches are available and, with a bit of luck, the fish and chip shop may be open. After lunch take the road going north out of Hawes towards Hardraw, the Buttertubs and Swaledale. A flagstone path crosses the fields near to this secondary road and is still part of the Pennine Way. Take the road bridge over the river Ure at grid ref. 877904, then look for a signpost on the right-hand side of the road which points the way across the fields to Sedbusk.

The afternoon walk from Hawes to Bainbridge is quite short, 12 kilometres, so to lengthen it and add more interest, it might be worthwhile taking a short diversion from the road bridge and following the Pennine Way to Hardraw village to see Hardraw Force. This may be approached only by way of the Green Dragon pub: a small fee is charged at the bar. Hardraw Force is the biggest unbroken waterfall in England above-ground. Everyone forgets about Gaping Gill because it is underground, but the latter has a total fall of 340 feet, though it is not unbroken. Hardraw Force is just less than 100 feet.

The falls at Hardraw were frozen from top to bottom in 1881.

A picture of this rather large icicle can be seen in the Green Dragon.

In 1899 torrential rain and hailstones on Great Shunnor Fell caused havoc at Hardraw.[5] Debris washed down into the valley and littered the fields behind the pub, and the bridge in the village was severely damaged. This happened on 12 July. A farmer who lived further up the valley was to have cut his hay that week, but after the storm his crop was buried beneath a foot of clay. The top of the falls was damaged by the storm and thus its shape was spoilt. The lip of the falls has since been reconstructed and so the present falls are not entirely natural.

From Sedbusk follow the minor road below the village which runs east and parallel with the Hardraw to Askrigg road. Do not take the road up to Litherskew at grid ref. 895911, but follow the path still parallel with the road to Shaw Cote; then take the path which bears north to Skell Gill at grid ref. 923915. The village is almost deserted as only one house is occupied. The owners are very friendly and were keen to show me their nineteenth-century fireplace and the picture of it in Marie Hartley and Joan Ingilby's book, *Life and Tradition in the Yorkshire Dales*.

Walk through the village, following the road to its junction with the road from Helm. Turn right and walk down the hill for about a quarter of a kilometre then turn left on to a well-defined path leading across the fields to Mill Gill. When you reach the wood the short diversion to Mill Gill is well worthwhile, particularly in the late spring when the wood is a sea of bluebells and later in the year is replaced by garlic: it smells lovely in this form, far better than suffering the smell second-hand from someone's breath!

These falls have also been known to freeze.

The corn miller used the force of water at Mill Gill to generate electricity as early as 1908.[3] So successful was he in his business venture that he supplied electricity to Askrigg, Aysgarth and Reeth in Swaledale until the national grid reached the Dales in 1948.

In 1799 Wordsworth described the idyllic approach to Mill Gill, in a letter to Coleridge. After the railway was built in 1877, the Victorians used to visit Askrigg by train for day trips to see Mill Gill and Whitfield Gill Force further upstream. Today, the latter is not so easily accessible.

The walk downstream from Mill Gill to Askrigg is very pleasant, and the path well maintained. It passes West Mill where corn was ground until after the First World War.

Many trades were followed in Askrigg. Over the years these have included farming, cheese and butter making, lead-mining and stonemasonry. The village was famous for its clockmakers. The first came from Halifax in about 1681. Several local men who followed suit became famous for their Grandfather clocks in their own right. The most prosperous tradesmen in Askrigg, however were the hand-knitters and the dyers. These trades were probably developed in about the middle of the sixteenth century; by the eighteenth century there were eleven families of dyers recorded in the parish registers. The hand-knitters and weavers of Wensleydale and Swaledale brought their goods to Askrigg to be dyed.[3]

When you reach Askrigg walk through the churchyard, which leads to a path across the field to the Askrigg to Bainbridge road. Turn right and follow the road a short distance to where it crosses Whity Gill coming from Mill Gill. Here a signpost points to the fields where a path follows a westerly direction behind the old railway station.

You are now very close to the site of Fors Abbey which was founded in 1145. A document at Byland Abbey, of which Fors was an offshoot, tells us that the Abbey was at a place called Dale Grange, and the area still bears that name today. The original building at Fors was wooden. After eleven years the monks moved to Jervaulx where the climate was milder and more suitable for growing crops.

Beyond the railway station the path follows the course of the disused railway line, finally coming out onto the road half a kilometre north of Bainbridge.

Bainbridge to Hawes	23 km	14½ miles
Hawes to Bainbridge (without the Hardraw diversion)	12 km	7½ miles
Total	35 km	22 miles

Shorter Alternative

Take the Bainbridge to Bardale Head and the Fleet Moss road as in the main walk, then follow the Roman road from grid ref. 863854 past Wether Fell and back to Bainbridge.

Bainbridge to Fleet Moss to Bainbridge	21 km	13¼ miles

References

1. F.R. Pearson, *Roman Yorkshire* (A. Brown & Sons Ltd, 1936)
2. Harry Speight, *Romantic Richmondshire* (Elliot Stock, 1897)
3. Marie Hartley and Joan Ingilby, *Yorkshire Village* (Dent, 1953)
4. Ella Pontefract, *Wensleydale*, First edn (Dent, 1936)
5. Barry Cockroft, *The Dale That Died* (Dent, 1975)
6. Marie Hartley and Joan Ingilby, *Life and Tradition in the Yorkshire Dales* (Dent, 1968)

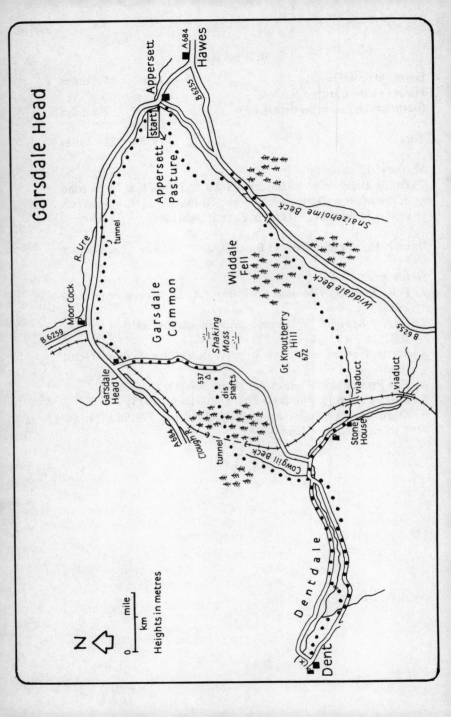

Walk 16: Garsdale Head

Appersett – Stone House – Dent – Garsdale Head – Appersett

42½ km (26½ miles) / 2,860 ft climb

SHORTER ALTERNATIVE
29 km (18 miles)

O.S.1 in 50,000, sheet 98: Wensleydale and
Wharfedale area

In Appersett a suitable parking place can be found near the bridge. Walk up the minor road from the bridge in a westerly direction to the disused railway line marked Bluebridge. Continue on the footpath in a south-westerly direction to the wood at grid ref. 839899. The path is not easy to follow and initially it may be necessary to take a compass bearing but the wood soon comes into sight and makes an easy point of reference. Follow this path across the footbridge at Widdale Beck (grid ref. 837890). Walk up to the B6255, turn right and walk south-west along the road for 1½ kilometres and cross the bridge over Widdale Beck at grid ref. 826878. Turn left, follow the footpath which starts beside the beck, then walk through the bottom of the wood and climb the saddle between Wold Fell and Great Knoutberry Hill. At the boundary wall grid ref. 795863 it is worth the one-kilometre diversion to go to the trig point on top of Great Knoutberry to see the view. Whernside, Dentdale, the Lake District hills, Wild Boar Fell and parts of Wensleydale can also be seen. Another path can be followed along another wall and back to the track which leads down Arten Gill to Stone House.

The viaduct is one of the many impressive features on the Settle to Carlisle railway.[1] The piers had to be sunk 55 feet into the ground in order to reach bedrock.

On a stretch of just 8 miles of this line the following engineering features can be seen:

Blea Moor Tunnel – 2629 yards long
Dent Head Viaduct – 199 yards long
Arten Gill Viaduct – 11 arches long and 117 feet high
Dent Station
Rise Hill Tunnel – 1213 yards long
Garsdale Station
Dandry Mire Viaduct – 12 arches long

The skill of the engineers who built this line is even more amazing when one remembers that it was built over a hundred years ago. The first passenger train ran on the line on 1 May 1876. A local Methodist preacher used to carry his bicycle through Blea Moor tunnel when he was going to preach at Dent as 'there was not much traffic on a Sunday'.

Follow the track below the viaduct to Stone House and turn right down the road. Even though the next kilometre is along a road, it is very pretty with the river Dee running alongside and the Sportsman's Arms an inviting stop; but I resisted and continued on to Dent. From Lea Yeat the Dales Way[2] follows paths on the south side of the road towards Dent. I preferred to stay on the road and admire the sweet-brier which were in full bloom in all shades from white to deep pink.

At grid ref. 719861 a signpost points the way along a footpath at the side of Deepdale Beck which joins the river Dee, and the path is well marked to Church Bridge at Dent. Dent is well worth a visit with its tall buildings and narrow cobbled streets – it gives the impression of having been by-passed by the twentieth century. The upper storeys of the buildings in Dent were used by the local knitters. Knitting in the Dales increased in the seventeenth century and reached its prime in the eighteenth century when large quantities of stockings were supplied to the army[3] and the trade continued into the early part of the twentieth century. All members of the family knitted, including the children. It was a means of supplementing the family income.

Dent's most famous son was Adam Sedgwick. He was born at the parsonage in Dent in 1785 and died in 1873. He was Woodwardian Professor of Geology at Cambridge and laid the foundation of modern geology.[4] A granite memorial to Sedgwick is situated in the main street of Dent.

There are two pubs in the village and excellent bar meals can be obtained.

From Dent return to Church Bridge and retrace your steps back to the road at grid ref. 719861 by the footpath following the River Dee and Deepdale Beck. After crossing the beck a signpost points the way across the field, up the hill and back to the river at grid ref. 725863. Cross the footbridge and turn right to the footbridge at grid ref. 732862; do not cross the river, but turn left and join the minor road running on the north side of the river Dee. Turn right, and walk just over 2 kilometres to a track leading off to the left which goes in a north-easterly direction with Cowgill Beck below it and to your right. Above a small wood the track is flanked by a stone wall, and eventually follows the edge of another wood not marked on earlier editions of the O.S.1 in 50,000 series. At the end of the wood, turn right and, following its perimeter, take the path which runs between a stone wall on your left and a wire fence on your right. This leads up to the air shaft for the tunnel at grid ref. 766890. Follow the path through the wood by the fire-break (compass bearing required) and join the minor road near Shaking Moss at grid ref. 786894. Turn left on the road and walk 2½ kilometres to Garsdale station. Just before you reach the station take a right turn and follow the perimeter of the wood again between a wall on your left and a wire fence. At the end of this short stretch of wood cross a stream; then go round the back of an embankment and drop down on to the disused Hawes branch of the railway at grid ref. 794922.

Garsdale station was the scene of a remarkable incident.[1,5] The trains making the long climb from Settle required assistance and so often two engines were coupled together. The extra engine was then uncoupled at Garside station and returned to Settle. This required a turntable to turn the engine round. On one occasion, whilst an engine was being turned round, the wind caught it and sent it spinning out of control. The engine was eventually stopped by pouring sand down the well. After this incident a stockade was built around the turntable to prevent a recurrence.

The viaduct in front of you is Dandry Mire viaduct. It was intended to be an embankment but, as the name suggests, it is on the site of a bog. Over a quarter of a million cubic yards of material was poured into this bog to make a firm foundation for the embankment.

Eventually the contractors built a viaduct instead.[1,5] There have been several fatalities on this line which are recalled in Barry Cockcroft's book.[5]

Once on the disused railway line you should not encounter problems with navigation. It is simply a matter of walking along the line to Appersett. There is one tunnel to negotiate above-ground. Walking is not easy because the hard core has been extracted from the line in places, leaving a rough stoney surface. A better route would be to come off the line at the entrance to the tunnel, (grid ref.821922). Walk down to the road, turn right towards Hawes, then after 300 metres take the small track to the right which eventually leads on to paths alongside the River Ure to Appersett.

Appersett to Dent	21½ km	13⅓ miles
Dent to Appersett	21 km	13 miles
Total	42½ km	26½ miles

Shorter Alternative
Apperset to Stone House (Sportsman's Arms) leaving out the climb of Great Knoutberry

	12 km	7½ miles

Stone House (Sportsman's Arms) down
the minor road to the farm track
leading up Cowgill Beck at grid ref.
754868, then route as above back to

Appersett	17 km	10½ miles
Total	29 km	18 miles

References

1. W.R.Mitchell and David Joy, *Settle–Carlisle Railway* (Dalesman,1976)
2. Colin Speakman, *The Dales Way* (Dalesman, 1979)
3. Marie Hartley and Joan Ingleby, *The Yorkshire Dales* (Dent, 1956)
4. Colin Speakman, *Adam Sedgwick* (Broadoak Press, 1982)
5. Barry Cockcroft, *The Dale That Died* (Dent, 1975)

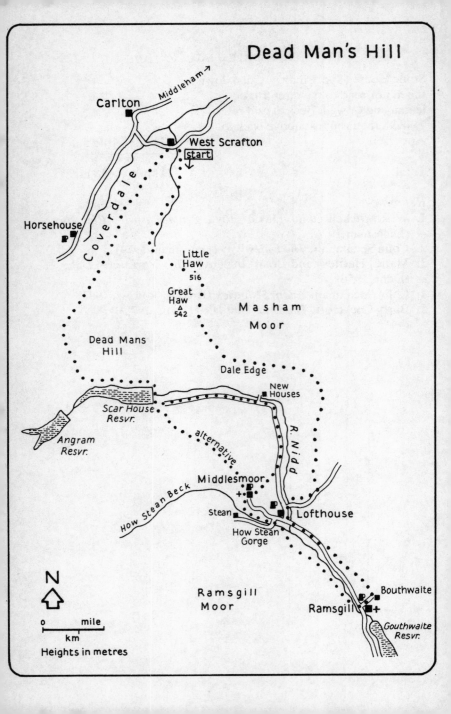

Walk 17: Dead Man's Hill

**West Scrafton – Little Haw – Dale Edge – Lofthouse –
Ramsgill – Scar House Reservoir – Dead Man's Hill –
West Scrafton**

35km (21¾ miles) / 2,200 ft climb or 2,600 ft if
returning via Middlesmoor

SHORTER ALTERNATIVE
18 km (11½ miles)

O.S. 1 in 50,000, sheet 99: Northallerton and Ripon
Area, or O.S. 1 in 25,000, Outdoor Leisure No 30:
Yorkshire Dales Northern and Central areas
All of the walk – apart from the last kilometre into
Ramsgill – is on the larger-scale map.

To drive to West Scrafton take the road up Coverdale from
Middleham, and park in the village. Near the village green the
road crosses a bridge over Great Gill. Immediately under the
bridge there is a pot hole, probably one of the lesser known
ones in the Dales. For this reason it is dangerous for children to
play in the stream.

A lady from a farmhouse nearby told us of an occasion when
a pot-holer emerged from the hole in the ground, and on seeing
the farmer's wife he said,'I wouldn't like to be you, missis.
There's two hundred foot of nought underneath your house!'

The meaning of the name Scrafton is 'the town by a hollow in
the earth'.[1]

Take the bridle-way heading south-south-east out of the
village and cross the watershed at Little Haw (grid ref. 080805).

Continue on this path past South Haw to its junction with the path skirting Dale Edge (grid ref. 089778). Here turn left (east) to follow the path, first east then south around the edge of the dale to shooting house, grid ref. 108754, then take either path for three-quarters of a kilometre to join the road from Lofthouse. Walk down the road into the village. From Lofthouse follow the road down-Dale out of the village for three-quarters of a kilometre to grid ref. 107730. Take the footpath through the field on the right that joins the course of the disused railway line then turn south to Ramsgill.

In monastic times Ramsgill was a grange of Byland Abbey and Bouthwaite nearby a grange of fountains.[2]

The Yorke Arms in Ramsgill is named after a local family. Sir John Yorke bought the Byland estates after the dissolution of the monasteries, and the mineral rights in the district were held by the family for 300 years.

After lunch at the Yorke Arms take the track along the west side of the river Nidd heading north-west and roughly parallel to the river, then follow the footpath to join the road at grid ref. 098733.

A shorter route is to follow the old railway track up Nidderdale to Scar House Reservoir. Or you can make a short diversion here and follow the road west-north-west for half a kilometre to How Stean Gorge. A small charge is made to walk through the gorge but it is well worth it. From the gorge take the path north-east to Middlesmoor, where Gouthwaite Reservoir can be seen 2½ miles down-dale beyond Ramsgill.

Follow the path out of Middlesmoor heading north-east to join the track of the light railway at grid ref. 099748.

This light railway was built in order to help in the construction of Angram and Scar House Reservoirs further up the dale.[3] Gouthwaite Reservoir was completed in 1901 but due to the increasing population of Bradford – in the years 1841 to 1891 the population had increased by 150,000 to 216,361 – there was a need for yet more water for the town. Bradford Corporation therefore set about building these new reservoirs. Railway construction started in 1904, the plan being to build a railway from Pateley Bridge to Scar House. This was completed and started running in 1907. In 1921 to 1922 during the height of its operations, the railway carried over 147,000 passengers – 106,000 workmen and 41,000 members of the public. A temporary village at Scar House which housed the workmen and their families had a population of 1,000 to 1,100. After the completion of the reservoirs in 1936 the stock of the railway was sold in 1937.

Follow the track of the railway up to Scar House reservoir. Walk across the dam at the east end of the reservoir. The scars on the hillside to the north are the quarries where the stone used in the building of the reservoir was mined. Follow the track in a westerly direction to grid ref. 047773 and turn right (north) to walk over Dead Man's Hill towards Coverdale. At grid ref. 048796 turn right to follow the bridle path back to West Scrafton.

West Scrafton to Ramsgill	16 km	10 miles
Ramsgill to West Scrafton	19 km	11¾ miles
Total	35 km	21¾ miles

Shorter Alternative
Starting from Ramsgill walk to How Stean Gorge and Middlesmoor north-west to Scar House Reservoir, then follow the river back to Ramsgill – about 11½ miles (18 km).

References
1. Ella Pontefract, *Wensleydale* (Dent, 1936)
2. Bernard Jennings (ed.), *A History of Nidderdale* (Advertiser Press, 1967)
3. D.J. Croft, *The Nidd Valley Light Railway* (Oakwood Press Second edn 1987)

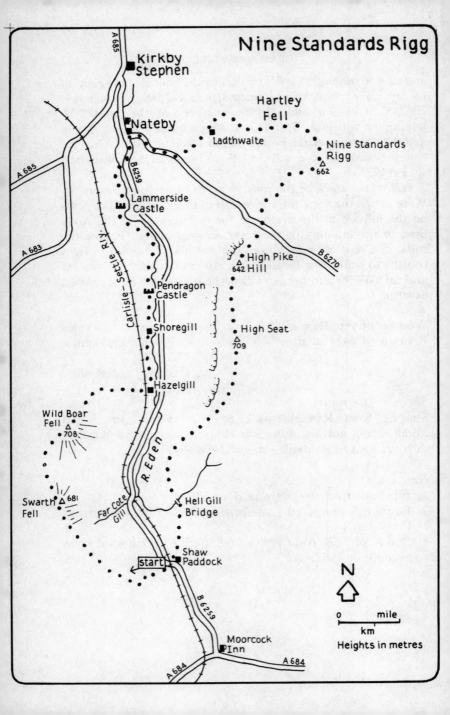

Walk 18: Nine Standards Rigg

**Shaw Paddock – Swarth Fell – Wild Boar Fell –
Hazelgill – Nateby – Nine Standards Rigg – Hell Gill
Bridge – Shaw Paddock**

Slight Variation of the Mallerstang Marathon

38½ km (24 miles) / 4,000 ft climb including six peaks
over 2,000 ft

SHORTER ALTERNATIVE
16 km (10 miles) / 1,900 ft climb

O.S. 1 in 50,000, sheet 98: Wensleydale and
Wharfedale area O.S. 1 in 50,000, sheet 91:
Appleby area

The Mallerstang Marathon is an annual event run from Shaw's
Youth Hostel: those competitors who stay at the hostel and
complete the event are awarded a certificate.

My route is very similar to that of the annual event, but I
have made slight alterations to the official route for two
reasons: one, to find a suitable place to park, and two, to
include a pub at the approximate half-way point. The route
from Nine Standards to High Pike Hill should only be
attempted in conditions of very good visibility.

Drive along the A684 from Hawes to Moor Cock then turn
right on to the B6259 towards Kirkby Stephen. About 2½
kilometres down the road is Shaw Paddock. Park the car on
the grass verge. From the north side of the hamlet, take the
path that goes under the railway in a direction of about 215°
towards White Birks Common. The footpath runs beside the
stream, which acts as a good guide to keep you on course.

Eventually you will see a cairn on the shoulder of Swarth Fell, but wait until you are clear of the boggy area before bearing right towards the cairn.

I did this walk one morning in mid-April after an overnight frost. As a result the boggy areas had a thin crust of frozen earth on them which was strong enough to hold my weight – in some places!

In *The Dale That Died*[1] Barry Cockcroft talks about the children from Grisdale going to school at Lunds 1½ miles over the fell on this path, but there were many days when they could not go because of the snow. 1902 was a particularly bad year. On returning from school the children had potatoes and a bit of bacon. It was a hard life living in the country in those days.

Follow the cairns up Swarth Fell and join the wall coming up from Holmes Moss where it turns at a right angle to cross the summit of the fell. The path is well-defined from the point at which you join the wall and makes for easy walking underfoot. Follow the wall over the top of Swarth Fell and down to a small tarn where the wall turns left, but the path up Wild Boar Fell continues straight ahead, heading for a cairn on the shoulder of Wild Boar Fell.

When you reach the plateau, instead of heading for the trig point take one of the other paths to the right in order to see magnificent views of Mallerstang Common from the edge. Wild Boar Fell gets its name from the fact that the last wild boar in England were hunted and shot there.[2]

The day I chose for this walk was perfect. The peaks of the Lake District were visible in the cold weather. Later in the day it was even possible to see Crifel in Scotland beyond the Solway Firth from High Pike, a distance of over sixty miles as the crow flies. The cold day afforded very clear visibility, and this was helped by a covering of snow on many of the peaks – no chance of a heat haze that day!

The descent of Wild Boar Fell from the plateau is most impressive as you look back towards the summit from the north, and that day in particular, as the snow gave the scene a Himalayan look.

The footpath down to Hazelgill is not well-defined and rather difficult to locate. A footbridge which crosses the Settle to Carlisle line is also difficult to find due to the steepness of the slope above it. Beyond the footbridge go past the farm to the river Eden, but do not cross it. Instead, turn left and walk downstream on the left bank of the river by the various footpaths, which are sometimes poorly defined, past Pendragon Castle and Lammerside Castle towards Wharton Hall.

Pendragon Castle is reputed to have been built by Uther Pendragon, father of King Arthur in AD 500, but the earliest factual evidence of it is from an inquisition dated the eighth year of Edward II's reign (1314), where it was mentioned by name.[3]. Lady Anne Clifford restored Pendragon Castle in 1660 and in 1663 she stayed at the castle after she made a journey from Skipton in her seventy-fourth year. Lammerside Castle was erected during the Border Wars between England and Scotland after the Battle of Bannockburn in 1314.

Take the bridge crossing the river Eden about 1 kilometre south of Wharton Hall and walk the final kilometre into Nateby along the B6259 road. Nateby is almost half-way and a convenient stopping place for lunch. After a couple of pints at its only pub, take the B6270 out of the village. After 1½ kilometres take a footpath on the left to Ladthwaite then turn right upstream, and strike up the hill to join the footpath on Hartley Fell going up Nine Standards Rigg. The summit of Nine Standards is not easy to find when climbing the hill, but an occasional glimpse of nine cairns grouped close together is confirmation that you are heading in the right direction. It would probably be easier to walk up the B6270 as far as the county boundary then to take the footpath on the left up Nine Standards Rigg.

From the trig point on Nine Standards, High Pike can be seen easily on a clear day (south-west direction) but if visibility is not that good it is unwise to even be attempting this walk. Take a footpath from the trig point to a cairn on the shoulder of the hill where the land drops away to a small gully. At this point a compass bearing is advisable to keep the correct direction when the route is not visible from the gully. I took my bearings on a small tarn in the general direction of High Pike. The reason for this was to pass round the right-hand side of the tarn. There were limestone clints on this side and it was therefore dry underfoot, as opposed to the left-hand side of the tarn which could be seen to consist of peat haggs.

After crossing the B6270 take the most direct route up High Pike. Although this is the steepest climb it is probably quicker: the last part of the steep climb can be completed in ten minutes.

Much of the route from Nine Standards to Hell Gill Bridge is ill-defined and therefore hard walking, the worst part being on Lamps Moss – but perhaps if I had found the path it would have been easier.

Once you are on High Pike the climbs are relatively easy and on a day of good visibility the next peak can be easily seen: these are High Seat and Hugh Seat, the latter being named after Sir Hugh de Morville of Pendragon Castle, who was involved in the murder of Thomas à Beckett at Canterbury Cathedral in 1170.[2]

From Hugh Seat turn east for the south end of Hangingstone Scar, then drop down to the Street, or Lady Anne's Way from where there is at last some easy walking to Hell Gill Bridge.

The Street starts at Cotter Riggs on the Hawes to Moorcock road, and until 1826 when the present road was completed, it was the only way out of Wensleydale to the north. The Street goes via Cotter End, High Dyke and Hell Gill Bridge, then drops down to cross the present road through Mallerstang at Deep Gill, and continues past Pendragon Castle and beyond. It was probably originally a primitive British track and it was certainly used by the Romans, because Hell Gill Bridge is claimed to be Roman in origin. In 1568, Mary Queen of Scots was escorted along this road to Bolton Castle where she was imprisoned, and Lady Anne Clifford travelled along this road in 1663 on her way from Nappa Hall to Pendragon Castle.[4] Hell Gill Bridge is worth a closer look, as it is one of only three Roman bridges still extant in the North Riding: Hell Gill Beck marked the boundary of the former North Riding of

Yorkshire and Westmorland.

It is worth taking a cautious look over the bridge to see the tiny beck tumbling under the bridge many feet below.

Follow the path which descends the hillside to Shaw Paddock.

This can be a very solitary walk, which adds to its charm. Swarth Fell and Wild Boar Fell are 'off the beaten track' for the Sunday afternoon stroller, and the second half of the walk can be even quieter. We met a man and his dog before climbing up Nine Standards Rigg, then not a living soul for over ten miles until we reached Hell Gill Bridge. There is little sign of man's presence in this area: I cannot recall passing any buildings, just an occasional wall, one metalled road and a few cairns. Even the sheep were few and far between. It is very gratifying to know that wild places can still be found in Britain in spite of the population explosion.

Shaw Paddock to Nateby	18½ km	11½ miles
Nateby to Shaw Paddock	20 km	12½ miles
Total	38½ km	24 miles

2,000 ft peaks

Swarth Fell	681 m	2,234 ft
Wild Boar Fell	708 m	2,323 ft
Nine Standards Rigg	662 m	2,172 ft
High Pike	642 m	2,106 ft
High Seat	709 m	2,328 ft
Hugh Seat	688 m	2,257 ft

Shorter Alternative

Take the route above from Shaw Paddock over Swarth Fell and Wild Boar Fell to Hazelgill (10½ kilometres) then follow the Street (Lady Anne's Way) back to Hell Gill Bridge and Shaw Paddock: 5½ kilometres.

Total	16 km	10 miles

References
1. Barry Cockcroft, *The Dale That Died* (Dent, 1975)
2. Norman Duerden, *Portrait of the Dales* (Hale, 1978)
3. Harry Speight, *Romantic Richmondshire* (Elliot Stock, 1897)
4. George C. Williamson, *Lady Anne Clifford* (Titus Wilson and Son, 1922).

Walk 19: Brandy Bottle Incline

Reeth – Barras End – Surrender Bridge – Old Gang – Great Pinseat – Whaw – Langthwaite – Hurst – Reeth

27½ km (17¼ miles) / 2,200 ft climb

SHORTER ALTERNATIVE
15km (9½ miles)

O.S. 1 in 50,000, sheet 98: Wensleydale and Wharfedale area. O.S. 1 in 50,000, sheet 92: Barnard Castle and Richmond area, or O.S. 1 in 25,000, Outdoor Leisure No. 30: Yorkshire Dales Northern and Central areas

Take the main road out of Reeth up Swaledale towards Muker. After the first corner out of Reeth take the first turn right (400 metres) up a sunken track to Riddings. Follow the track to the open moor, keeping the stone wall on your left. Where the wall drops downhill to your left follow the track leading straight ahead, keeping Calver Hill on your right; this track goes to Barras End at grid ref. 992009, sheet 92. This is the water-splash which was made famous by the television series of James Herriott. At the water-splash turn left and walk down the road for 1 kilometre to Surrender Bridge (grid ref. 989999, sheet 98). This is the bridge across Barney Beck which to the west of the bridge, is known as Hard Level Gill. On the 1 in 50,000 O.S. map the name Surrender Bridge does not appear, but according to local legend the nearby Surrender Moss derives its name from the fact that supporters of Bonnie Prince Charlie surrendered here, a story which I have been unable to verify in print.

Brandy Bottle Incline

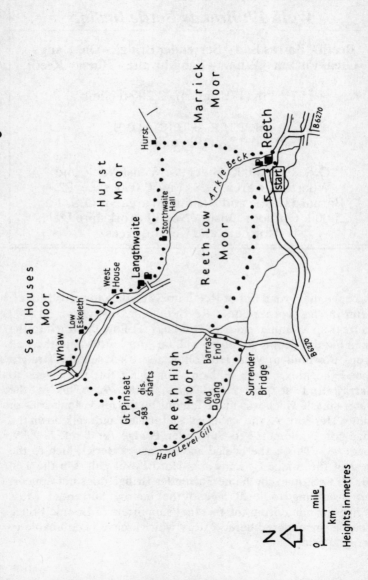

The ruined building downstream from Surrender Bridge is Surrender Smelt Mill. This and Old Gang smelt mill 1½ kilometres upstream from the bridge, were the principal smelt mills of the district serving the local lead-mines. A Dr Robinson practising in Reeth in the early nineteenth century noticed that 'the chronic epidemic of the district mental and physical was mining'.[1] This shows that the toxic effects of exposure to lead were known in those days.

From Surrender Bridge turn right and follow the path upstream past Old Gang smelt mills (grid ref. 976006, sheet 92).

On the moors to the right of Old Gang smelt mills there are the ruins of the peat house. A mixture of peat and coal was used for smelting the lead and the peat could only be cut in one month of the year, due to the wet climate, so the peat store had to be capable of holding a year's supply of the fuel, hence the peat house was very large: 391 feet long and 21 feet wide. The structure consisted of stone piers supporting a thatched roof.[1]

Continue along this track to the point on the map marked Level House, and where the track divides go straight ahead, not left. After half a kilometre the entrance to Brandy Bottle Incline can be seen on your right. The entrance is now filled in to prevent accidents. It originally provided an access point to Hard Level, which at this point runs roughly underneath the present path and on to Friarfold Rake which was once the most productive seam of lead in Swaledale, the seam following a south-west to north-east direction and joining up with the seams in Gunnerside Gill to the west.[2]

In the 1780s Hard Level was originally called Force Level. But it proved hard to drive, costing as it did about ten pounds a fathom; thus its name was changed to Hard Level.[3,4]

After Brandy Bottle Incline the track turns north and north-east. It eventually peters out due to recent working of the waste tips. Head towards a wall on the left and follow the wall to the trig point on top of Great Pinseat. This is hard to find because it is on the far side of the wall, which partly hides it.

From the trig point walk on a compass bearing towards

Whaw in Arkengarthdale. The village itself cannot be seen from here, but there are prominent land marks to follow. Although the going underfoot is initially quite rough, it does not last long and, once you crest the brow of the hill, you come across more waste tips from the lead-mining area and it is easy to pick up a path that takes you down to Whaw.

Cross Arkle Beck into the village, then follow the path by the beck into Langthwaite, which was famous in the introductory shots to the James Herriot series on television. Make the most of the pub: it is the only one on this walk. After lunch follow the path downstream on the east side of the beck to Storthwaite Hall, then turn left and go uphill following the path to Hurst at grid ref. 046023, sheet 92.

When on Hurst Moor I always think about the Roman pig of lead found here in 1885 by the miners[1] and one automatically finds oneself looking for another pig of lead.[1]

On reaching the metalled road in Hurst turn right (south) on to a path which goes through the mine tips with a chimney on your right. This leads to Fremington Edge, where you suddenly come upon a magnificent view of Reeth. This view is worthwhile compensation for not finding that Roman pig of lead.

Follow the path down to Fremington, then walk back into Reeth.

Reeth to Langthwaite	18 km	11¼ miles
Langthwaite to Reeth	9½ km	6 miles
Total	27½ km	17¼ miles

Shorter Alternative

Follow the route from Reeth to Barras End as above, then walk north up the minor road to Bouldershaw House for three-quarters of a kilometre. Then take the track down to the road near Arkle Town at grid ref. 007019, sheet 92; turn left and walk half a kilometre up the road to Langthwaite.

From Langthwaite follow the waymarked path by the side of Arkle Beck back to Reeth.

Reeth to Langthwaite	8½ km	5¼ miles
Langthwaite to Reeth	6½ km	4 miles
Total	15 km	9½ miles

References

1. Robert Clough, *The Lead Smelting Mills of the Yorkshire Dales and Northern Pennines*, Second edn (Clough, 1980)
2. Arthur Raistrick, *The Lead Industry of Wensleydale and Swaledale*, Volume 1: *The Mines* (Moorland, 1975)
3. Arthur Raistrick and Bernard Jennings, *A History of Lead Mining in the Pennines* (Longman, 1965)
4. R. Fieldhouse and B. Jennings, *A History of Richmond and Swaledale* (Phillimore, 1978).

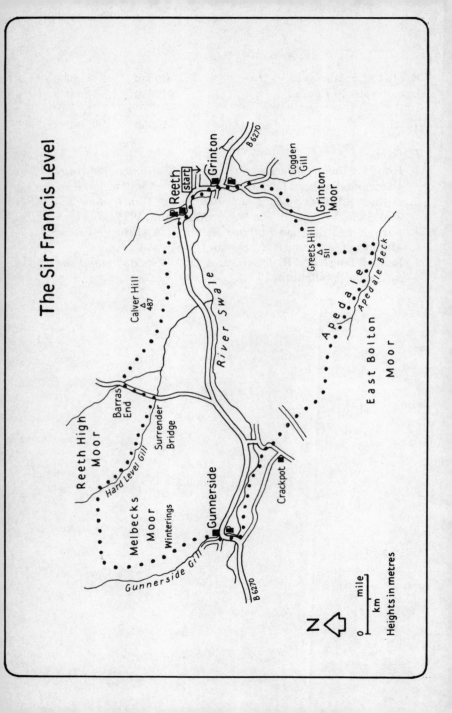

The Sir Francis Level

Walk 20: The Sir Francis Level

Reeth – Grinton – Greets Hill – Apedale – Gunnerside – Gunnerside Gill – Surrender Bridge – Barras End – Reeth

33½ km (21miles) / 3,000 ft climb

SHORTER ALTERNATIVE
21½ km (13½ miles)

O.S. 1 in 50,000, sheet 98: Wensleydale and Wharfedale area. O.S. 1 in 50,000, Sheet 92: Barnard Castle and Richmond area, or O.S. 1 in 25,000, Outdoor Leisure No 30: Yorkshire Dales Northern and Central areas

The most convenient place to begin this walk is at either Reeth or Gunnerside because in both of these villages there is plenty of space to park. In Grinton, on the other hand, it is difficult to find a parking place.

Park on the green in Reeth. Walk through the village on the B6270 towards Grinton. Cross the bridge over Arkle Beck then take the waymarked path through the fields to the right. This brings you out on to the road at the bridge over the Swale in Grinton.

The main building of historical interest in Grinton is the church, parts of which date back to Norman times. The bowl of the font is Norman. Grinton church was the only church in the upper dale until Muker church was built in 1580.[1] Prior to this date the dead were carried from the upper dale by the Corpse Way to be buried in consecrated ground at Grinton. They were brought from as far afield as Keld to Grinton church. A wicker basket was used to carry the body instead of a coffin, because the basket was lighter. The funeral cortège consisted of the pall-bearers and the family and friends of the dead man. As many as two hundred people would attend a service before the procession began.[2] On the journey down-dale the guests lived at the expense of the bereaved.

The Queen's Head in Muker, now a private house, was an overnight stopping-place for the funeral cortège. The relatives of the dead paid the landlord for drinks for those attending. They drank out of special funeral mugs.

On the journey down-dale the pall bearers would naturally have needed to rest occasionally, and the body in its wicker basket would be laid down on a long flat stone. These were the 'coffin stones'. One such stone can be seen on the north side of the river at Ivelet Bridge.

There were various branches of the Corpse Way in Swaledale, depending on where the deceased had died. From Keld, the Corpse Way goes over Kisden, heads towards Muker, then turns left to cross the Swale by a ford near the present footbridge. It continues past Calvert Houses to Gunnerside, and up on to the hillside on the track going down-dale and parallel to, but above, the present road running along Swaledale. Above Feetham are the foundations of a building known as the 'dead house'. The wicker basket containing the deceased was left here whilst the cortège went to the Punch Bowl at Low Row for refreshments. From Feetham the Corpse Way passed through Kearton and Healaugh to Grinton.

A further branch of the Corpse Way crossed Ivelet Bridge and followed tracks south of the river; passing Gunnerside, continuing to Harkerside and finally arriving in Grinton.

After the consecration of the cemetery at Muker in 1580, those who died in the upper dale, above Gunnerside, were buried at Muker, and those who died below Gunnerside were still buried at Grinton; thus the Corpse Way continued to be used.

The Corpse Way provides yet another example of the various origins of the green tracks and footpaths in the Dales, and is evidence that the church at Grinton was central to the life of the whole of Upper Swaledale.

From the church walk up the minor road heading south and, at the first road junction, take the left-hand fork to Grinton Lodge, now a youth hostel. This was the setting for Lowood Institution in the 1970s film version of *Jane Eyre*.

The lead-mines in the Grinton area are first recorded in 1219.[3] The area to the west of Grinton Lodge is still known as the Smeltings and according to Arthur Raistrick[4] this is because the lead from the mines was smelted in the nearby Bail Hills. There is no evidence here of Roman mining, but it is thought that the Brigantes mined lead in the Grinton area for several centuries prior to the Romans.[3]

From Grinton Lodge walk up the road 1 kilometre to the bridge over Cogden Gill where you leave the road, and follow the Gill for about half a kilometre to the ruins of the smelt mill.

The present building is thought to have been erected in about 1820-1822[4] but that it replaced a much older smelt mill on the same site. The original mill was probably built by the owner of the Grinton mines, Humphrey Wharton, in 1628. The shell of the building is well-preserved, as it has been used for farming purposes for many years. The smaller room on the north side of the building housed the water-wheel which Arthur Raistrick deduces was 18–20 feet in diameter. A hole in the wall of this room indicates the height of the watercourse that powered the wheel. Originally, bellows were driven by the water-wheel but later they were replaced by a blowing machine. This consisted of an upright cylinder containing water, in the centre of which was a pipe extending above the height of the water. Above this was a smaller cylinder, driven by the water-wheel and reciprocating, thereby acting as a piston to drive air down the pipe where it was fed to the ore hearths. The larger room of the building contained three ore hearths.

The most productive days of Grinton smelt mill were probably before it was rebuilt in the 1820s. In 1768 the mill was particularly busy. At that time sixteen horses were employed to carry the ore from a mine in the Whitaside group to be smelted at Grinton.[3] A close look at the O.S. map indicates several paths in the vicinity of the smelt mill that may have originally served as pack-horse routes between the lead-mines and the various smelting mills. The smelt mill was worked until 1893.[4]

Just below the smelt mill there is a stream that joins Cogden Gill from the west. Follow the path along this stream – it is marked by hatching on the O.S. map – to where the bridle-way from Greets Hill joins the minor road over Grinton Moor at grid ref. 038963. The hatchings on the map indicate areas where the surface of the ground has been worked for lead. The sheer size of these excavations indicates the great magnitude of man's activities in lead-mining in the past.

The open circles on the O.S. map, which are a feature of this area of Grinton Moor, and make it look as if the map has got measles, are the locations of bell pits, one of the early techniques of mining, whereby a hole was dug down to the seam of lead.

When you reach the road a signpost indicates the direction to Greets Hill. The waste heaps act as a good guide, but all the same it is best to take a compass bearing.

An old quarry on Greets Hill was in use during the eighteenth and nineteenth centuries, the stone from which was in great demand; in fact it was used by Walter Morrison to build Malham Tarn House which replaced an earlier hunting lodge. It is now used as a field centre.[5]

Follow the track from Greets Hill down into Apedale. This section of the track was built up and roughly metalled so as to be able to bear the heavy loads coming from the stone quarry. At the junction of the tracks in Apedale (grid ref. 031942) turn right and follow the track going up the dale. This valley was a location of intense mining activity, and a map in Arthur Raistrick's book shows the main vein of lead in the valley closely following the course of the present path up the dale.[5]

Above Apedale Head one passes over the watershed and back into Swaledale. Take the more westerly of the two tracks to the minor road at grid ref. 983964, then go down the farm lane in a north-westerly direction. At the point where this joins another farm lane at right-angles follow the path marked on the map to the bridge over the Swale at grid ref. 977974. Do not cross over the Swale but turn left and follow the minor track on the south side of the Swale which goes west to join the main road at Hag Wood (grid ref. 949977); then walk the half kilometre north on the road into Gunnerside and find the King's Head.

After lunch there are two alternative routes up Gunnerside Gill: either go straight up the Gill on the footpath opposite the pub or take the path halfway up the valley side that passes below Winterings Scar. We chose the latter, mainly because the low-level path by the Gill is not too easy underfoot. We also did this walk in the last week in October when it was cold, and the best way to warm up was to climb the hillside in order to get the heart pumping faster.

The higher route up Gunnerside Gill is approached by leaving the village on the main road going east; when you have passed some houses by a tap set into the wall take the track to the left, and at the first junction take the left-hand metalled path. This goes past Bents, Potting, Whin Hall, and Winterings, so named because it is the lower-lying, sheltered pasture where the sheep grazed in wintertime. The cliff face above and to the right is Winterings Scar, above which have been found traces of several Bayle Hill smelting sites.

At the base of the valley and in line with Winterings Scar is the Sir Francis Level, named after Sir Francis Denys son of Sir George Denys a local mining engineer. The idea was to drive a level parallel to the gill in the direction of Blakethwaite so that the level would undercut the rich veins of lead that crossed the valley a mile further north. In this way the mining area would be drained and so serve as another means of access to the mines. After a careful survey to confirm the depth at which the level would undercut the various veins, the level was begun in 1864. Progress was very slow: the first part was cut at a rate of 10 feet a month.[6] Only two men at a time could work on the advancing face, as there was so little room. They worked for two six-hour shifts a day. Even in the softer ground, the rate of progress was only 20 feet a month. Later, rock drills were used:[5] These were powered by a water-wheel 38-foot in diameter which compressed air to give a supply at 60 lbs/in^2. After 1873 dynamite was used, and this speeded up the rate of driving so much that by 1877 the Friarfold vein had been cut. The normal lease for a mine was 21 years, so apart from the expense of driving the level, it was very time-consuming and did not allow the mining company much time to reap the benefit of its labours. Large quantities of ore were extracted from the various veins served by the Sir Francis Level, so much so that it was economical for the company to build two crushing mills at the entrance to the level. The ore was brought from the veins by the Sir Francis Level to the surface where it was crushed and dressed, then taken above-ground up the Gill to Bunting Level, where it was passed into the hard level complex. It was then carried underground to the Old Gang Smelt Mill. This was far cheaper than transporting the dressed ore over the top of the hill to Old Gang.

A hydraulic pumping engine was installed 43 fathoms below-ground on the Sir Francis level. This was powered by water from Sun Hush Dam 1 mile away on Ivelet Moor. The 50-horsepower engine worked pumps and a hoist and is still in position underground today.[5]

From Winterings follow the track up Gunnerside Gill and look out for the large scars on the far side of the valley. These are hushes dug out by the early lead-miners to extract the lead ore. The two hushes you will see are Sun Hush and North Hush. A recurring feature of the hushes is that they often have a shaft sunk into them to extract the lead ore from greater depths; at a later date usually in the eighteenth century although they had a limited use in Roman times, a level was driven into the hillside to drain the seam and extract more ore. The level at the bottom of North Hush is known as Priscilla: it extends 1,000 yards into the hillside. On the moor above the Hush was Sun Hush Dam. Water was collected in a dam such as this on the high moor above a seam of lead outcropping on the steep slopes of a hill. When a large volume of water had collected, the dam was breached to release a flood of water down the hillside. This carried debris with it and so uncovered the lead mineral which the miners then dug out. The hillside opposite contains all of these features associated with the lead-mining activities: the early hush with the dam above it, a shaft, and a level driven into the bottom of the hush.

The east side of the gill also has many hushes cut into it. It is hard to believe that these large features of the landscape are man-made. Their size indicates the extent of the mining activities over the years, and the richness of the veins.

The walk now leaves Gunnerside Gill and follows the track over Melbecks Moor to Hard Level Gill. This requires some skill in map-reading as the early part of the track striking up the hillside is not easy to find, but if you aim for the saddle between the two higher points of Melbecks Moor this should lead you on to the well-defined track.

The tops are like a lunar landscape with the remains of waste heaps all around. These waste heaps have been reworked in modern times to reclaim some of the minerals that were left behind by the lead-miners. Fluorite, a valuable source of fluorine and barytes, or heavy spar (barium sulphate) are both associated minerals, and are often found with galena, the mineral of lead.

Where the track reaches Hard Level Gill at grid ref. 964014, you will see Level House marked on the map at grid ref. 963014. This house was occupied in 1692 by Adam Barker; a partner and manager in some of the mines[4] and parish records indicate that in 1744 'Mary, the daughter of John Borras, of Level House' was christened.[3] I have passed this point several times but have not seen any signs of the house.

About a mile downstream from Level House one comes to the ruins of one of the most famous smelt mills in the Dales: Old Gang smelt mill. A short distance upstream from Old Gang on the right-hand side of the track you will see the entrance to Hard Level. This level played a key role in the activities at Old Gang. It was started in 1785 by Lord Pomfret. The idea was to link up the mine workings in Gunnerside Gill with the Old Gang complex. In order to do this a level was driven from Gunnerside Gill. This was known as Bunton, or Bunting Level. By this means the two rich veins of Old Rake and Friarfold were reached. However, the level from Old Gang, (initially called Force Level) proved to be very slow in progressing, so its name was changed to Hard Level and the name of the gill also changed, from Old Gang Beck to Hard Level Gill.

The transport of lead ore underground from Gunnerside Gill to Old Gang has already been mentioned. This came through the Hard Level. The importance of this area can be appreciated by examining the records, which show that in the five years from 1839-1843 the Hard Level, Bunting and Brandy Bottle (half a kilometre above Level House on Hard Level Gill) areas produced over 10,000 tons of lead.[6] There is no documentation of the mine before the eighteenth century.

The lead ore from Hard Level was smelted at Old Gang. There are two mines at the site. It was common practice to use materials from a former mill to build a new one, and it is such a mill that can be seen today. It dates from after 1828, but there was a mill here in 1771.[5]

Although the production of Old Gang in years prior to 1875 exceeded 2,000 tons annually, it rapidly dropped to less than 500 tons by 1880, and by 1885 production had almost ceased.[4]

The peat store is behind and above the mill. The peat was usually only dry enough to cut in one month of the year, so the store had to be large enough to hold a year's supply of peat: hence the great size of this building. It had end walls and piers between to support the framework of the roof, which was thatched. The building had open sides and was 391 feet long and 21 feet wide. The end walls and piers are still in position.

Leaving Old Gang, walk down the gill from Old Gang past the waste tips. At a point mid-way between Old Gang and Surrender Bridge you pass the remains of another mill, but this is hard to spot. This was once the High Mill belonging to Sir Thomas Wharton, and it was active in 1680.[4] Continue walking downstream to the point where Hard Level Gill goes under the minor road at Surrender Bridge (grid ref. 988999, sheet 98). If you continue on the track running parallel to the stream for 100 metres or so, the ruins of Surrender smelt mill soon come into sight but the best view of the mill is from the other side of the stream on the road coming up from Healaugh. The first mill at Surrender was built in 1669 but it was replaced by another mill in 1839. Robert Clough[3] quotes from the contract: 'The lessees were at liberty to pull down the old mill, using what material they wished for the new mill.'

The original mill had a chequered career. Between 1808 and 1813 when lead prices were high the mill produced £72,500-worth of lead at a cost of £75,000.[6] This was due to the fact that the mill stood on a high plateau: hence some of the ore had to be raised a total of 220 fathoms (1,320 ft). The Surrender mines, which supplied ore for smelting to the Surrender mills, prospered in the mid-nineteenth century but by 1870 production of the smelt mill had dropped to 70 tons and the mill ceased to operate in 1880.

Leave Surrender Bridge by walking north up the minor road for one kilometre to Barras End. After crossing the stream take the footpath heading south-east, which passes Calver Hill (sheet 92) and finally comes down to Riddings at grid ref. 027997, sheet 98, then take the road into Reeth.

Gunnerside is the approximate half-way point so if it is used as a lunchtime break, the morning and afternoon walks will be about the same distance.

Reeth to Gunnerside	16¾ km	10½ miles
Gunnerside to Reeth	16¾ km	10½ miles
Total	33½ km	21 miles

Shorter Alternative

Starting at Reeth follow the same route as above through Grinton, Grinton smelt mill, Greets Hill and Apedale and down to the bridge over the Swale just west of Low Row. Then follow the minor track running east on the south side of the river to Low Whita Bridge and continue eastwards on the footpath which leads to a footbridge over the Swale and into Reeth.

Total   21½ km   13½ miles

References
1. Ella Pontefract, *Swaledale* First edn, (Dent, 1934)
2. Edmund Cooper, *A History of Swaledale* (Dalesman, 1973)
3. Robert Clough, *The Lead Smelting Mills of the Yorkshire Dales And Northern Pennines* Second edn, (Clough, 1980)
4. Arthur Raistrick, *The Lead Industry of Wensleydale and Swaledale*, Volume 2: *The Smelting Mills* (Moorland, 1975)
5. Arthur Raistrick, *The Lead Industry of Wensleydale and Swaledale*, Volume 1: *The Mine* (Moorland, 1975)
6. R. Fieldhouse and B. Jennings, *A History of Richmond and Swaledale* (Phillimore, 1978)

Walk 21: Tan Hill

Gunnerside – Muker – Keld – Tan Hill – Raven Seat – Keld – Gunnerside

33½ km (21miles) / 2,850 ft climb

SHORTER ALTERNATIVES
1. 24½ km (15¼ miles)
2. 17½ km (11 miles)

O.S. 1 in 50,000, sheet 92: Barnard Castle and Richmond area. O.S. 1 in 50,000, sheet 98: Wensleydale and Wharfedale area, or O.S. 1 in 25,000, Outdoor Leisure No 30: Yorkshire Dales Northern and Central areas

Park in Gunnerside, walk east up the minor road to Dyke Heads and past Calvert House. Continue on this road, which eventually becomes a footpath, to Muker footbridge at grid ref. 910986. Cross the bridge and double back to follow the path to Muker, where there is a post office general stores and a pub, the Farmer's Arms. Take the lane out of Muker that leads to the hamlet of Kisdon (grid ref. 904986). You are now on the Pennine Way and at the highest point about 800 feet above the valley bottom. In a lead-mine at Arn Gill on the opposite side of the valley four miners discovered a vein of lead which made them £400 in eight weeks. The task of dividing the money equally amongst them was beyond their capabilities mathematically, until one of the men borrowed a pint measure from the Queen's Head in Muker and their problem was soon solved.[1]

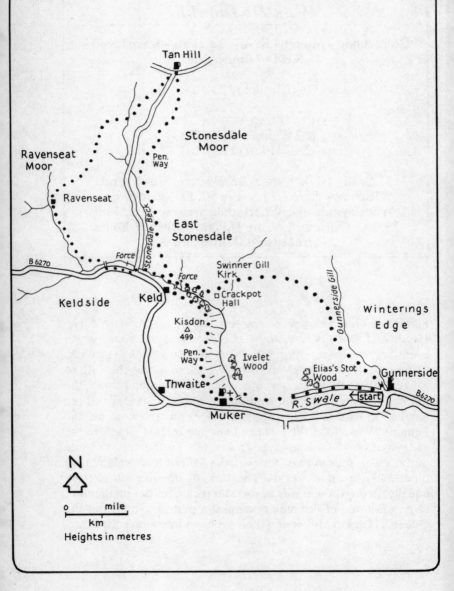

Tan Hill

Ravenseat Moor

Ravenseat

Tan Hill

Stonesdale Moor

Pen. Way

Stonesdale Beck

East Stonesdale

B 6270

Force

Force

Keldside

Keld

Swinner Gill Kirk

Crackpot Hall

Gunnerside Gill

Winterings Edge

Kisdon △ 499

Pen. Way

Ivelet Wood

Elias's Stot Wood

Gunnerside

B6270

Thwaite

Muker

R. Swale

start

N

0 mile
km

Heights in metres

Follow the Pennine Way north round Kisdon Hill towards
Keld but before you reach the village cross the footbridge over
the Swale at grid ref. 896012, sheet 92 and follow the Pennine
Way north to Tan Hill at grid ref. 897067, sheet 92.

Tan Hill is the highest pub in England. It used to be in
Yorkshire until Edward Heath gave it to Durham in the county
boundary reorganization – you can't trust these southerners!
The pub is now only open during the summer months, so it
might be advisable to telephone and check the day before you
go to avoid disappointment.

When you come out of the pub turn west and follow the road
for a few metres, then take the left turn to West Stonesdale, and
follow the road for about a quarter of a kilometre to an outcrop
of rock on the right-hand side. Take a compass bearing for
Raven Seat at grid ref. 863033. If you avoid the obviously boggy
parts it is easy walking underfoot. There is just a chance you
may find the path, but it is unlikely, as it has not been in regular
use since the end of the lead-mining era nearly a hundred years
ago. Besides, it gives one a sense of achievement to mount the
top of the hill and to see from the compass bearing that one is
right on course.

At Raven Seat, keeping to the east side of Whitsundale Beck,
follow the waymarks back to the Swale at Smithy Holme
Bridge, (grid ref. 878017, sheet 92). Cross the bridge and turn
east onto the B6270 for one kilometre, then take the road to the
left up West Stonesdale and over the river. After a steep climb
take the first right-hand turn down a minor road, which leads
you back to Keld footbridge. At the bridge, follow the path on
the north side of the river Swale to Crackpot Hall (grid ref.
907009, sheet 92). Take the path behind the Hall heading
towards the junction of Swinner Gill with East Grain Gill (grid
ref. 912012, sheet 92). The area behind Crackpot Hall was once
the site of Beldi Hill lead-mines, and was the subject of a
disputed ownership in the eighteenth century.[2,3] The result was
that water used to dress the lead ore was instead directed down
one of the shafts with the intention of 'watering out' the men in
the mine.

Further up the gill you will find Swinner Gill Kirk. This is a cave near the waterfall where non-conformists held services in the seventeenth century. They chose remote places because if they were caught they were fined. A look-out would be posted nearby to warn of the approach of the authorities.[4]

Take the path up East Grain Gill in a general easterly direction. Before you reach Gunnerside Gill turn south-east on the path to the position marked shooting box at grid ref. 934006, and continue on this path in a general southerly direction to Dyke Heads and back to Gunnerside.

Gunnerside to Tan Hill	16 km	10 miles
Tan Hill to Gunnerside	17½ km	11 miles
Total	33½ km	21 miles

Shorter Alternatives

1. Start and finish at Muker (part route as above)

Muker to Tan Hill	10½ km	6½ miles
Tan Hill to Muker	14 km	8¾ miles
Total	24½ km	15¼ miles

2. Start and finish in Keld (part route as above).

Keld to Tan Hill	7 km	4½ miles
Tan Hill to Raven Seat to Keld	10½ km	6½ miles
Total	17½km	11 miles

References
1. Edmund Cooper, *Muker – The Story of a Yorkshire Parish* (The Dalesman, 1948)
2. Arthur Raistrick, *The Lead Industry of Wensleydale and Swaledale*, Volume 1: *The Mines* (Moorland, 1975)
3. Arthur Raistrick and Bernard Jennings, *The History of Lead Mining in the Pennines* (Longman, 1965)
4. Ella Pontefract, *Swaledale*, First edn (Dent, 1934).

Afterword: Walking and the Country Code

Walking is one of the finest forms of exercise, and is enjoyed by a large majority of the population. It caters for all levels of fitness, from the convalescent to the very fit competing in endurance events.

Most people take up walking as a hobby in order to spend their leisure time in the country, and what better place to start than in the Yorkshire Dales?

As one becomes more enthusiastic about the country one is eager to learn more about it. This naturally leads to a greater awareness of such varied subjects as: archaeology, industrial archaeology, local history, flora and fauna, farming, geology, meteorology, ecology, etc.

Even the most rudimentary knowledge of any of these topics will give greater satisfaction when walking in the country.

If the walker is to continue to have access to the country, it is important that we don't get a 'bad press' with those who live and work there: for this reason always obey the Country Code:

> Guard against all risk of fire.
> Fasten all gates.
> Keep dogs under control.
> Keep to the paths across farmland.
> Avoid damaging fences, hedges and walls.
> Leave no litter.
> Safeguard water supplies.
> Protect wildlife, wild plants, and trees.
> Go carefully on country roads.
> Respect the life of the countryside.

Bon Voyage!

Index